STORM SPLITTER

STORM SPLITTER

HILLIARD LAWRENCE LACKEY

STORM SPLITTER

KJV
Scripture quotations from the Holy Bible, King James Version (Authorized Version). First published in 1611. Quoted from the KJV Classic Reference Bible.

iUniverse books may be ordered through booksellers or by contacting:

iUniverse
1663 Liberty Drive
Bloomington, IN 47403
www.iuniverse.com
1-800-Authors (1-800-288-4677)

ISBN: 978-1-5320-5566-9 (sc)
ISBN: 978-1-5320-5567-6 (e)

Library of Congress Control Number: 2019914828

Print information available on the last page.

iUniverse rev. date: 09/23/2019

To fellow former sharecroppers, as honored by the Cotton Pickers of America Monument and Interpretive Center in Mound Bayou, Mississippi.

And to all those on Garmon Farms in rural Quitman County during the summer of 1957. It was they who labored with me, worshipped with me, and of course shared experiences in and out of the cotton fields with me.

CONTENTS

FOREWORD

by Dr. Joseph Martin Stevenson

My heart is deeply warmed whenever native Mississippians write about their homeland. This is especially so when natives of the Mississippi Delta put pen to paper, recalling the days of yore, when sharecropping had supplanted slavery as the peculiar institution. My friend and colleague Hilliard Lackey is as deeply imbued with the history, culture, and legacy of the Mississippi Delta as anyone. This book takes literary license to blend facts and fiction but generally describes Delta life in 1957.

Personally, I am delighted that Brother Lackey is passing along the sharecropper tale about splitting a storm. Whether such actually happened, I don't know. But I do know that Delta senior citizens, to this day, can weave yarns about storm splitting, apparitions (hants), and many other bone-chilling stories. We need more firsthand written accounts, stories, diaries, and other recollections of Delta life by ordinary people. I have always contended that ordinary people have extraordinary stories to tell. The story lines may be simple, but graphic descriptions reflecting time and place are invaluable.

As this *Storm Splitter* story unfolds, the reader gets an unusual look at the plight of 1957 sharecroppers forced into service as day labor cotton choppers by the Soil Bank Act of 1956. No longer allowed to have their own half-share crops, tenant farmers became day laborers.

The Soil Bank Act—Title I of the Agricultural Act of 1956 (P.L. 84-540)—created the Acreage Reserve Program to retire land producing basic commodities under an annual agreement from 1956 through 1959, and the Conservation Reserve Program to retire agricultural land under contracts of three, five, or ten years. The Soil Bank Act was repealed by the Food and Agriculture Act of 1965 (P.L. 89-321, Sec. 601).

PREFACE

I am the son of sharecroppers in rural Quitman County near Marks, Mississippi. I am the fourth of eleven children: seven boys, four girls. My most interesting year on the planation was 1957 as I approached my fifteenth birthday. I was the designated water boy for cotton-chopping day laborers. That was a special time in my life and in America, as the Soil Bank Act of 1956 paid plantation owners not to plant cotton. The longstanding practice of working on the halves (the planter and the tenant split the profits, as calculated by the planter—sharecropping) was put on hold.

Undaunted, erstwhile sharecroppers became day laborers and took to cotton chopping at thirty cents an hour, ten hours per day, for five and a half days a week. We tried really hard to earn $16.50 every week. Only a heavy rain or thunderstorm could stop us. Or could it? Could a storm split into halves with an open, clear space in the middle, allowing cotton choppers to continue? Would the honor of splitting the storm fall to a saint or sinner? As plantation water boy, I had a firsthand view.

The National Oceanic and Atmospheric Administration (NOAA) describes a thunderstorm that splits into two storms that follow diverging paths—a left mover and a right mover. The left mover typically moves faster than the original storm; the right mover, slower. Of the two, the left mover is most likely to weaken and dissipate (but on rare occasions can become a severe anticyclonic-rotating storm), while the right mover is the one most likely to reach supercell status.

African slaves coming to the Americas by way of the Middle Passage brought with them a deep-seated belief that approaching storms could be diverted by piercing Mother Earth with an ax. The prevailing belief was rooted in the West African occult that the resident shaman, witch doctors, or holy men under whatever name wielded power to protect villages or field workers from devastating storms.

Among African Americans in the South, this tradition fell to the most spiritual elderly men and sometimes women of a community. Following emancipation and transgressing years, the practice dissipated into hardly believed fables. Occasionally, in the middle of the twentieth century, a relic of the past could be found, one who still believed in and practiced the craft of storm splitting.

Usually, the intervener was highly spiritual and saintly in nature and an acknowledged man of God. Dolph Rhodes, an Albino hoe filer, a bootlegger on a Delta plantation, was none of the above. Yet amid a cotton-chopping crew led by the head deacon of the community church, and with several mothers of that same church looking on, Dolph Rhodes split an oncoming thunderous black cloud into north and south segments. Or did he? If he did, why would God select him and not the head deacon? Why weren't the mothers of the church anointed to do God's bidding?

In the midst of various and sundry other cotton field dramas, the prevailing thread is that God utilized the services of a well-known sinner to save cotton choppers from an impending storm. The plot thickens when the community's most revered church deacon challenges the sinner man to a standoff to ascertain which of them could divert the next incoming storm.

This is a work of fiction, not a memoir, but the content accurately reflects life in the Mississippi Delta in 1957. Admittedly, much of what is written is based on lived experiences. Drama, romance, comedy, and acculturation took place in the cotton fields. Going to work in the fields was like listening to or watching a soap opera. I cringe at memories of how intriguing and sometimes harrowing planation life was like in those days.

Storm Splitting

Picture this: A dark cloud is approaching from the west. Thunder is rolling in the distance. Lightning flashes on the horizon. A telltale stillness hangs in the air as the barometric pressure steadily ebbs. A storm is imminent. Suddenly, a grim-faced black man emerges with a double-bladed ax and stands in front of the house facing west, looking into the teeth of the storm. Muttering something under his breath, he raises the ax and in a dramatic downward swoop sinks the front blade of the ax into the ground. The approaching thunderstorm arrives but amazingly splits into southern and northern segments, leaving the path carved by the embedded ax free from overcast skies.

Poppycock. Preposterous, you say? Only folklore. Witchcraft. Hoodoo. Maybe voodoo. Say what you will, call it what you want, but there are many among the elderly who witnessed or heard tell of storm splitting. Granted, such eyewitness accounts are becoming rather rare, as only those who are in the seventy-to-ninety-year-old age bracket seem to have primary evidence. Those who are younger only testify to hearsay.

There hasn't been any recent accounting of storm splitting. Maybe the practice has run its course. Maybe the double-bladed ax is becoming obsolete. Maybe the ax wielder is a dying breed. Maybe, just maybe, science and technology have undercut the belief in the effectiveness of storm splitting. For whatever reason, storm splitting appears to be a thing of the past. More important, it actually happened—and happened often in the Deep South within African American communities until at least the 1950s.

There is no readily found documentation of storms being split in mainstream history narratives. That doesn't mean storms were never split. In fact, there are many observations of storms splitting or going around given locations. The only question is whether such going around was caused by forces of nature or heralded by human intervention.

Amazingly, the *American Meteorological Society Online Journal* (volume 35, issue 10, October 1978) carries documentation that storms can and do split for scientific reasons. The following is about a man-made experiment concocted in a laboratory.

> We have used a three-dimensional cloud model to investigate the splitting of an initially isolated storm in a one-directional east-west shear. The simulated evolution of storm splitting in some cases follows all four stages suggested by Achtemeier (1969) after analysis of radar data, including the development of two self-sustaining storms. One of these storms moves to the right of the mean wind vector and the other to the left.

The question remains: Was there any correlation between sinking an ax into the ground and the actual splitting of storms? Logic says no. Eyewitness and hearsay take the opposite view. Several books on Deep South folklore have notations about storm splitting based on oral history gleaned from aging African Americans.

The *Handbook of Texas Online*, "Folk Belief," carries this brief but explicit statement: "An axe stuck in the ground can 'split the cloud' to prevent an unwanted storm."

Newbell Niles Puckett has written extensively about the southern Negro's penchant for sinking an ax into the soil to divert the path of an approaching thunderhead. Puckett contends that the practice was a mainstay of West Africans and was retained by African Americans for centuries before Westernization and integration of the 1960s rendered it passé.

The novel by Ray B. Browne, *A Night with Hants and Other Alabama Folklore Experiences*, has an interesting passage on page 75 where a mother directs her teenage son to "Get out there, take that double-bladed axe and split that storm." There is no mistaking that storm splitting is frequently noted in African American folklore. *Merriam-Webster* defines *folklore* as "traditional customs, tales, sayings, dances, or art forms preserved among a people." Other cultures relate stories of Paul Bunyan, Babe the Blue Ox, John Henry the Steel Driving Man, and even Moses crossing the Red Sea.

Strom splitting is a stable in African American folklore. Whether or not there was a causal relationship between plunging a double-bladed (double-bit) ax into the ground in the face of an oncoming dark cloud and the subsequent division of that cloud into southern and northern segments may never be proven. However, eyewitness accounts tell us that it really and truly happened.

CHAPTER 1

THE ALBINO SINNER

My chest was burning as my lungs heaved desperately for fresh air, the salt twinge of sweat running down my forehead, seeping into bugged eyes. Yet I ran and ran and ran, faster and faster. Behind me stood thirty-two anxious hoe hands leaning on their hoes and Papa Mike sitting just inside the door of the Chevrolet carrier truck. All eyes were on the runner, me, the water boy, sent to fetch the double-bit ax.

My chest heaved, and my legs ached. My heart raced. The thunder grew louder and louder. The storm would be on us in minutes.

I neared the tin-top, frame shotgun house situated atop a rise just off the road. Behind the house, and between the house and the chicken coop, was the woodpile of split oak and sweet gum. Dolph Rhodes had said it would be there. "There it is," I said aloud and was shocked to hear myself wheezing. I was finally there. I made the final, near-exhausted steps into the backyard.

It was a double-bladed ax, freshly sharpened on both sides. Like his brother, Eddie Rhodes could put an edge on a blade. Word was out that he carried a switchblade knife and a straight razor in addition to a .38.

I stared at the double-bit ax for a moment and then looked around for some sort of carrying case. Seeing none, I grabbed the ax and was in motion again.

1

I ran back to the turn road, up the turn road, and then down through ankle-high cotton to Dolph Rhodes. I handed the ax to the squat albino with dark glasses.

Dolph Rhodes was a quiet man who walked with a shuffle and a limp. He wore shades—dark glasses—day and night. He had been born without pigmentation in the outer layer of his skin. He was an albino child of a black mother and a black daddy as far as anyone knew. More than that, he was different. Dolph Rhodes was a self-acknowledged, unpretentious sinner. Never one to feign affection or hypocritical status, he was always the same: gambling-house operator, moonshine whiskey salesman, and hoe filer for day hands on Garmon Farms.

On this day, in the face of an approaching storm, Dolph Rhodes was acting like a holy man from the motherland. Without saying, he was going through the motions as if he had been anointed to split a storm with a double-bit ax. Traditionally, this was a role reserved for the most pious of men—men who were saintly in nature, who fasted and prayed in preparation for the occasion. Dolph Rhodes was giving the appearance that he could split an oncoming storm with a double-bit ax without portfolio. He was self-appointed and not anointed.

The dark, billowing clouds were blowing across the top of a line of cypress trees in the southwest. The sky looked like bruised skin. Dark clouds were rolling like tumbleweeds in a cowboy movie. Some say that if you see yellow or green around the edge of a storm, you're going to have hail. Birds had vacated the area. Gnats, flies, everything was gone. Everybody and everything was quiet. No one was talking except Old Man Turner. "I told y'all that if it thunders 'fore seven, it will rain before 'leven. It's almost 'leven."

Someone said, "Ol' Man, it's ten o'clock in the morning."

A terrible thunderstorm was rushing toward us, but the air was still. The downdrafts, cold air being sucked from aloft to the ground, were driving away the sweltering heat as the storm approached. It felt eerily different. I was scared. The thirty-two hoe hands in Papa Mike's crew were not in agreement about what to do. The seventeen teenagers and youth wanted to bolt for shelter. The couple, Rayford and Ollie Mae, and their three female buddies were wavering. It was the cluster of older choppers led by Mama Rosetta that wanted to snatch the ax from Dolph Rhodes and let Papa Mike lower the ax in the face of the storm.

Mama Rosetta was tall, just like her husband, the crew chief. They could easily have been brother and sister. They had been married for forty-three years, pillars of the community, trusted overseers of black cotton choppers. Papa Mike was the first man among black day laborers. Mama Rosetta was first lady. She knew it. Everybody knew it.

"Don't move, y'all. Peace. Be still. Let Jesus work through my husband." The words quivered out of her mouth, as she was sure her husband had sent for the ax.

Gasping for breath, I sucked in air and handed the ax to Dolph Rhodes.

Mama Rosetta, ever the micromanager, hollered out in a reprimanding tone, "Jesus, boy, give the ax to Papa Mike! That storm's 'bout to kill us!"

Before I could react to Mama Rosetta, Dolph Rhodes firmly gripped the ax. I looked worriedly over at Mama Rosetta, to Papa Mike, and finally back to the ax-wielding Dolph Rhodes. I took two, three, and then four steps backward, stumbling over a cotton row, angling in the general direction of my mother and younger brother. This was getting scarier and more surreal with each passing moment. There, I had said another of those reading words to myself: *surreal*. At a time like this, I was thinking strange words and definitions gleaned from reading the family dictionary.

Dolph Rhodes squared his squat, overall-covered body at a right angle in the path of the oncoming clouds, sparkling periodically with lightning flashes. Temperatures were falling fast. Old Man Will Tanner, limping on his elevated left shoe, broke the stony silence with a line from Charles Albert Tindley's "Stand by Me": "When the storms of life are raging!"

As if on cue, Dolph Rhodes lifted the double-bladed ax with the polished hickory handle and held it high above his head. I trembled in fear as the sky darkened to the color of coal. Suddenly, a tremendous bolt of lightning seared down. Dolph Rhodes plunged the ax into deep Delta topsoil. Usually, the hoe filer spoke in low, even tones—barely above a whisper. This time, he exalted an audible "Haaaaaaah" following his ground-piercing penetration. Simultaneously, the loudest clap of thunder I had ever heard shook the ground. Everyone fell to the ground, some writhing in anxiety, some still with faces in hands, as fear gripped everybody.

Until this day, no two eyewitnesses among the thirty-two hoe hands heard or saw the same thing. I must say—I have also related differing accounts of what happened next.

Some say lightning struck the shining stainless steel blade on its downward plunge. Others say the ax flashed in reflecting the glow from the lightning. Still others say the ax flew through the air in a shining glide, split the topsoil, and mired itself handle deep in Mississippi gumbo.

They all agreed on the rest. The loudest clap of thunder ever heard ensued, rolling and crackling through the afternoon sky like tons of dynamite. Mama Rosetta fell to the ground like cut spruce. Almost on cue, everybody reacted to the astoundingly loud thunder and either fell flat or knelt on the ground. The noise was deafening.

The bolt cut a deep swath in the cotton field. The air smelled a mixture of scorched shoe leather, smoldering embers in a mosquito smoke bucket, and the burning carcass of a dead mule.

In an instant, it was over.

I was flat on my stomach, down between two cotton rows. Slowly, I got up on my knees, looked around, and cautiously rose to my feet. Something drew my attention skyward. Looking up, I was astonished to see blue skies above, not the dark, violent swirl of an angry storm.

Dolph Rhodes had stood his ground. His eyes covered by dark glasses, he reached in his right back pocket for his red-and-white-polka-dot handkerchief. With the finality of a fait accompli, he wiped his brow, pointed to me, pointed to the ax, and pointed to the house on the ridge. He then turned and began sauntering nonchalantly to the Chevrolet carrier truck where his soft drink carton and hoe files were stashed.

The sky above the cotton field was blue. To the north and to the south were torrential downpours. The storm had taken a V shape, coming as one massive white-speckled dark cloud with lightning, laden with heavy rain but parting and detouring on both sides of the double-bit ax and the thirty-two hoe hands.

Nobody was laughing. Nobody was clapping. Mama Rosetta was praising Jesus, and a few of her mother board sisters were chiming in with her. Everybody else was just plain old awestruck.

"Did you see that?"

"Did you see what I saw?"

"Did I see that?"

Dolph Rhodes had split the wind with a double-bit ax.

I looked over and saw that Mama and my younger brother Billy were all right. Papa Mike worked the ax handle from its perch in the gumbo dirt and walked it back to the woodpile. I wondered to myself what had just happened.

The day had started with nothing out of the ordinary. There was no harbinger of things to come.

"Ah-ah-achoo! Ah-ah-achoo! Ah-ah-achoo!" That was Mama sneezing in the kitchen. She always did that when sprinkling black pepper in the large skillet filled to the brim with six scrambled eggs. Now, the pungent aroma of strips of lean pork frying was distinguishable. Rice, eggs, and homemade bacon with cat-head biscuits comprised weekday breakfast.

Mornings during cotton-shopping time were predictable. Daddy was up and outside around four in the morning. He carried his and Mom's chamber pot to the outhouse, gathered eggs from the chicken coop, scattered kernels of corn on the ground for the chickens, slopped the hogs, and ostensibly used the outhouse himself. He was always up and about, always busy doing something meaningful for the family.

Mom used to make the fire in the woodstove and start breakfast. That changed last fall when my brother and I saved up eighty-six dollars over two years and bought a gas range.

Uncles Frank and Jerry Anderson, although just four years my senior, had two years earlier in 1955 secretively stashed $1,100 and bought a Dodge car, paid in full. Allegedly, they hid dollar bills from their weekly tractor-driving income into an iron bedpost at the foot of their aged, green-spotted bedpost. Each side of the bed they shared had a post with a removable cover atop. Each twin uncle had put equal amounts into each side week after week, month after month, and year after year until they reached $1,200. Then they called all the extended family together one Saturday morning to show and tell as they each took a coat hanger and fished out their side of the bedpost. They were given a ride to Clarksdale, and they came driving back in the newly purchased but used four-door Dodge sedan.

Suffice it to say, young minds, old minds—everybody for miles around was talking about where and how the twins had saved $1,200 and paid $1,100 cash for a car of their own. People started looking into bedposts at the twins' home, everybody else's home, and their own homes, searching for a stash of cash. None was ever reported.

My then thirteen-year-old brother, Billy, and I had decided to stash some cash and buy a gas range to eliminate the chore of getting firewood every night just after dark. Plus, Mama wouldn't have to make the fire before cooking. Our efforts were not clandestine or cloaked in any secrecy. We told everybody that we were saving the funds. Having no bank or credit union, we allowed Old Man Allen Walsh to hoard our loot. Strange, no one thought about either parent stashing the cash. It just seemed natural to ask Mr. Walsh. After all, he was known to carry and hoard cash income from collecting burial insurance premiums. We were determined to raise eighty-six dollars, and that we did.

I was lying there smiling to myself for taking part in the money-saving campaign that led to removing that wood-cutting stumbling block. Brothers Billy, age thirteen, Sam, age ten, Charles, eight, and Earl, five, all shared the middle room with me. Billy, baby boy Earl, and I shared the big bed. Charles and Sam had the small daybed. That was the bed that big brother James (Bob) used to have before he left home at age sixteen in 1955 to live with my late father's brother in Saint Louis. He was now at Lackland Air Force Base in San Antonio, Texas. Bob came home every now and then, talking big stuff about how he had his own bed in the air force. Surely, he jests. How in the world did they have enough for hundreds, even thousands of young men to have their very own bed?

The two sisters had the front room of the modified shotgun house—that is, a house in a straight line from front to back. It started with a combination living room and parents' bedroom up front. The middle two rooms housed girls, and the next boys. Finally, a kitchen was at the back. That room used to belong to Mama and Daddy before a side room was added just off the front room. Daddy was a World War II veteran and had used the Servicemen's Readjustment Act (GI Bill) of 1944 to learn carpentry at Delta Trade in Clarksdale. He could build houses, let alone add a room to a house. So, with the help of friends and with lumber provided by Garmon Farms, the new room had taken shape and become the parents' bedroom.

Sisters Barbara Jean, age eleven, and baby girl Shirley Ann, two, had the room all to themselves. Big sis Carrie, age twenty-three, had married and flown the coop years before. Cora, age sixteen, also known as Dimp, had just finished high school, and in search of self-betterment, she accepted Uncle L. S.'s invitation to live with his family and work in Saint Louis.

Cotton was planted in early to mid-April after the last killing frost. Nowadays, cotton seeds are dropped, planted with two or three in the same space. In those days, the seeds came out in a long, steady stream, requiring cotton choppers to chop a space between the seedlings soon after they emerged from the ground. A mature cotton stalk needs six inches from its neighboring stalk to grow and bear its precious cotton bolls.

The merging cotton seedling also needs to be free of stifling weeds and grass. Crab grass, Bermuda grass, and other competing plants were afoot. This required three choppings. The first was to chop a space between plants and rid it of any encroaching grasses or weeds. The second chopping came in late April or early May when the cotton stalks reached six to ten inches high. This did away with any grasses and weeds that the plows had not reached. A third foray through the cotton fields was needed when the cotton stalks were near maturity but rains might have caused clumps of grasses or weeds to grow in low places. This was breezy, just-before-lay-by-time cotton chopping in late May or early June. July and August were lay-by time. That's when black children went back to school.

School was out from Easter through the Fourth of July and from Labor Day through Thanksgiving. School was in session from Thanksgiving to Easter, with a break for Christmas. A summer session was held in July and August.

I loved to wake up around four when Daddy came through the room. No, I didn't want to get up—just be awake and slumber, drifting in and out of consciousness for an hour or so. This was a time to preplay the day's activities. I had this habit of reviewing the day before falling asleep at night and previewing the following day before rising. The pastor said that God held his children accountable for their deeds, weighing the good against the evil, so I was determined to hold myself accountable.

On this particular morning, I was reflecting on the storm being split, God, Mr. Dolph, and Papa Mike. The pieces of this puzzle just didn't seem to fit right. The storm, the saint, the sinner, and the results were all controlled by God. The saint ought to have been the hero.

Mama sounded out the warning signal: "All right, y'all can start stirring about. Breakfast will be ready in ten minutes." The radio was on WDIA, as usual. She turned it on every day at 5:00 a.m. sharp.

Theo "Bless My Bones" Wade was playing his sign-off song by the Angelic Gospel Singers "In the Morning When the Dark Clouds Roll Away." That meant 5:29 a.m. and the start of Early Morning Blues Show with A. C. "Moohaw" Williams at 5:30 a.m. The blues theme song was instrumental with voice-overs by Moohaw that said in part, "So, Mr. Freddy, if you are ready, get up!" I always wanted my feet to hit the floor before Moohaw said the words "get up." Although broadcasting from Memphis, WDIA was the lifeblood of the North Mississippi Delta.

With that strong signal beaming from Memphis down into the Mississippi Delta's dense African American population (the signal reached from the boot heel of Missouri to the Gulf coast), WDIA was able to reach 10 percent of the total African American population in the United States.

The broadcasters seemed like family: Nat D. Williams, Robert "Honey Boy" Thomas, A. C. "Moohaw" Williams, Ford Nelson, Rufus Thomas, Robert "Honeymoon" Garner, Martha Jean "the Queen" Steinberg, Reverend Dwight "Gate Mouth" Moore, Maurice "Hot Rod" Hulbert, and special messages from owner Bert Ferguson.

The cotton-chopping truck would be stopping out front at 5:50 a.m. Time to move and move fast; use it, wash your face, eat your breakfast, and get your hoe.

A frenzy of activities ensued in the twenty minutes between 5:30 and 5:50. Everybody age ten and up caught the truck for the cotton fields. The girls used their chamber pot, also known as a slop jar, in the privacy of their room. My brothers and I sprinted for the outhouse, with the winner going inside and the losers taking the bushes and nearside family cotton rows abutting our house for makeshift restrooms.

Hurriedly, everyone made their way to the back porch to wash up, meaning face and hands, in a portable face bowl and a foot tub. To dry our hands and faces, we used a faded-gray, once-white-but-now-dingy communal towel hanging on a clothesline. Full-body bathing in a number 3 tub was reserved for Saturday afternoons or Saturday nights. Washing feet before bedtime in a foot tub, a number 2 tub, was the norm. Brushing teeth with an old toothbrush and Arm and Hammer baking soda was not routine but an intermittent endeavor. Chewing sweet gum twigs was more routine for cleaning teeth and fighting tooth decay.

To an outside observer, the scramble to the breakfast table might have seemed chaotic and out of control. But to the family, it was a well-oiled machine at its best. Within ten minutes, everybody was situated and ready for prayer and grace. There was a 36 × 60–inch rectangular table with wooden benches on each side. Daddy led prayer, usually the Lord's Prayer.

The rest of us jockeyed for position to say grace, usually in a round robin from oldest to youngest, with the thrill being whether the youngest could remember:

God is great and God is good,
And we thank him for our food.
By his hand we must be fed.
Give us, Lord, our daily bread.
Amen.

We ate rice, eggs, and homemade bacon in five to eight minutes, with little small talk. To say breakfast was gulped down is an understatement. Looking back, this could very well be a primary source of the family's history of stomach ailments. Eating hurriedly, hardly masticating food, puts tremendous pressure on the digestive tract. The military would have been proud of this family. Breakfast was a breeze in terms of time.

Age ten was the line of demarcation separating stay-home children from new farmhand children. Those who stayed home had to have a babysitter. At age eight, that lot fell to Charles this year. Sam had aged out of babysitting and at age ten was ready for cotton chopping. Charles had to take care of Earl and baby Shirley Ann. The rest had to catch the truck.

How Mama fixed breakfast, fed us, and still caught the truck is a mystery whose secret is known only to Delta area mothers of that time. Some people say that black women are the pack mules of Western civilization. Assuredly, women like Mama carried the heavy load for the lifestyle of the Mississippi Delta. They cooked, cleaned, nursed, mothered, wifed, birthed, labored, churched, raised, reared, chopped, picked, pulled, buried, and everything else with an *-ed* on it.

"Heah come the truck!" It was 5:51 a.m. The morning ritual was over. It was time to hit the field and begin ten hours of hard labor chopping cotton. The day was divided into five-hour shifts from 6:00 a.m. until 11:00 a.m. and 1:00 p.m. until 6:00 p.m. That left two hours for lunch, known colloquially as dinner.

"The truck is out there!"

Mama was giving Charles directives as she pulled on her long-sleeved shirt, put on her straw hat, and picked up her brown gloves with the fingertips out. "Charles, boy, watch them peas; don't let the juice get too low. Pour in a cup of water at eight and ten. Feed Earl and Shirley at seven. Y'all stay out of the road now. Watch out for them speeding cars, trucks, and things."

Daddy was moving in a dog trot, heading the half mile toward the shop where the tractor drivers and day laborers gathered for their daily assignments at six o'clock. He would be on time.

A new episode was unfolding as everybody scurried to the truck, leaving Charles, Earl, and Shirley at home alone. This was going to be some kind of day.

CHAPTER 2

BIRDS OF A FEATHER

Mama Rosetta, Katie Randolph, Mamie Lyons, Lovie Parsons, Anna Jones, Minnie Plunk, Dinah Lyons, and Clyde Thomas formed one cluster of cotton choppers among the twenty-five to forty under Papa Mike's supervision. Today there were thirty-two. Another day, especially following a rain, there could be forty or more. Men driving tractors chopped cotton when fields were too soggy for the heavy tractors. Papa Mike could always find a spot high enough to be dry enough for cotton chopping.

The older crowd led by Mama Rosetta was the fastest-moving cluster. They began chopping minutes before the 6:00 a.m. starting time, before Papa Mike could say, "Here we go." They started out front and stayed out front all day, every day, from Monday morning until Saturday noon.

There were four other groups: mothers with children six through ten or eleven; young married couples or young grown people; teenagers; and grown men tractor drivers on temporary assignments.

Mothers with children usually brought up the rear as the teaching-learning process in the art of cotton chopping slowly unfolded.

Birds of a feather flock together, as they say. Cotton choppers among day laborers tended to be like the birds. They cordoned themselves according to eye-ranged interest.

The hoe filer and water boy proved to be what bound groups together. Dolph Rhodes filed the hoes (ubiquitous blades attached to the end of a rounded shaft). Most hoes had sixty-inch handles. The shorter version was fifty-two inches. The blade had a quarter-inch edge that needing sharpening two to four times a day. Dolph Rhodes could renew an edge on a blade with the best of sharpeners. His shuffling limp, dark glasses, and drooping bottom lip made him a trademark. There was one drawback: he refused to carry gossip, words of warning, or any other information from group to group. He was a nonentity or mere fly on the wall while slowly working his way among the categories of workers during the course of a day. I was a fine specimen of a teenager compared to the much older, droopy-shouldered Dolph Rhodes, even though I was a bit gangly. I was blessed with a gift for gab, and I fancied myself the self-appointed promoter of peace and harmony among Papa Mike's cotton choppers. I guess you could say I was an ombudsman, an arbiter, a floating ambassador. I relished the thought of cotton chopping being a harmonious gathering of old and young, male and female.

On this midafternoon following the storm, stunned onlookers resumed cotton chopping while buzzing about the ax that split the wind.

The mothers and children group was curious. Grown women were trying to convince growing youngsters that God had acted through Dolph Rhodes to split the storm. Growing youngsters were doing their best to make moms understand that Dolph Rhodes and Moses had a lot in common. One split the Red Sea, and the other split a storm.

Teenagers are skeptical by nature. They question everything. This is divine providence's way of assuring that progress is constant. Each succeeding generation looks with unabashed scrutiny at the preceding generation's icons and treasures. They discard and accept with abandonment. On this midafternoon, the establishment had faced an oncoming storm with some voodoo-based notion that an ax could somehow divert the path of the billowing, dark clouds. Unbelievers, disbelievers, and skeptics; those were before words. The after words were more like, "That couldn't have happened, could it?"

Dee Dee and Cookie were sisters. They had a black-and-white television set at home, the only TV in a black home in the community. They had seen their share of Hollywood magic. This was outdoors, right in front of their eyes. This was awesome. Dee Dee and Cookie were scared.

Carl and Mable were brother and sister. Both were splendid physical specimens, born a year apart. She was fifteen. He was fourteen. Her growth spurt during puberty had made her physically equal to him. They looked like fraternal twins: strong bones, muscular features, and high energy.

The events of the last few minutes had given rise to brightened excitement. Carl was stuttering at fever pitch. "Can't, can't, can't, can't, no, no, no, no, no, ax spli, spli split, no-no-no, stor, stor, storm can, can, can, can, it, wa, wa, Water Boy?" His eyes were wide, his countenance aghast as he struggled with words and even more so with doubt and acceptance of what he had witnessed. Carl wanted relief.

Before I could utter one word and put in my two cents' worth, Mable spoke in the unmistakable condescending tone big sisters have used to discredit little brothers since time immemorial. "Boy, shut your stupid mouth. You can't talk. Now, you can't see. Blind Bottommost knows Mr. Dolph split the storm. Shut up and chop."

I had to laugh at that take-charge statement. I smiled knowingly at Mable and turned with compassion to Carl, the erstwhile Joker. I tried using logic. "Two things happened at the same time. Mr. Dolph swung the ax, and the storm split. It's like the rooster crowing and the sun rising. It's like the road grater smoothing the rocks on the gravel road, and the rain comes. It's just the way you look at it."

Cupcake, Dee Dee, and Cookie's younger sister seemed impressed by my apparent wisdom. At age thirteen, Cupcake was a newcomer to the teenage cluster. She had been around me before but had, to my knowledge, paid little or no attention to my wit. I was to learn much later that Cupcake had heard her father mention several times that I had a lot of intellect. Yet their church was down at Woodlands, while my family attended Friendship. Hearing me explain the most perplexing incident of her young life was impressive. Plus, I guess she ascribed some degree of importance to me as a participant in the storm-splitting episode. These things apparently aroused a strange stirring inside her. She spoke quietly, the words seeming to come from some far place. "Would you repeat that again for me? I am confused."

Frowning at her use of "repeat" and "again" in the same context, I straightened my five-eleven, 140-pound frame and with a bucktoothed smile retorted, "When two incidents occur at the same, they are called co-incidents. Did one cause the other? Did they just happen at the same time? That's the question."

Cupcake was coming back to reality now. She hadn't heard or understood anything. I sensed she just wanted my undivided attention. She spoke again, this time recognizing her voice. "Will you give me a drink of water in my own cup? I don't drink behind snuff dippers."

Seizing the moment, I obliged. The water was shade-tree cool but without ice. The ice man seldom came around during overcast weather. Besides, the thermometer on the side of the carrier truck had slid down to eighty-three degrees, a full fifteen degrees lower than it was before the storm.

Cupcake filled her retractable cup and, sporting red fingernails, sipped water while her big brown eyes smiled at me. I got the impression that she'd made up her thirteen-year-old mind to challenge me. She seemed to shiver at the prospect. Suddenly feeling uncomfortable in her presence, I moved on with the water bucket in my right hand and the long-handled metal dipper in the left. Short-haired, vertically challenged, puberty girls just didn't appeal to me. My eyes were elsewhere—perhaps misplaced but nonetheless elsewhere.

Her name was Ollie Mae. She was a bit above medium height, about five six, with long hair, a full bosom, brown skin, and the roundest, most protruding backside I had ever seen. She must have been twenty-three or twenty-four years old.

Ollie Mae had moved into the community in late March, just before the end of school. She was full of fun and loved to dance by herself down at Little Sister's Juke Joint on Saturday nights.

She had pizzazz. She became instantly familiar, as if you'd known her all your life. Old men thought about younger days. Young men panted and plotted. Boys wanted to be men right away. One thing was wrong. Ollie Mae was married to Rayford.

Rayford was jet black, lanky, and medium height, with flashy white teeth. He liked to wear a dingy white shirt hanging on the outside of his trousers, with the collar open two or three buttons below the neck. Rayford had Ollie Mae if nothing else. This seemed to please him to no end. He was arrogant and cocky and got stumbling drunk every Saturday night. Boys and men alike wished Rayford would drink himself into a blackout. Ollie Mae would be free, a toss-up. It never happened.

I shifted my straw hat on my head to hide coveting eyes as I approached Ollie Mae, Rayford, Mattie Lee, and the other married or might-as-well-be-married groupies. A gust of wind blew the straw hat clean off my head and sent it tumbling over and over, back toward Papa Mike.

I didn't want anybody, especially Ollie Mae, to see me blush. The outline of her very rounded, extremely protruding backside would have been visible from under the rim of the straw hat. Just the sight of that automatically made me uneasy. Yet I couldn't take my eyes off her backside until she turned to me. Her voice was sweet like violins, warm like a calf's breath, yet seemingly as forbidden as homemade sin. Goose pumps rose on my arms. I was flustered.

"Boy, where is your straw hat? Just 'cause it cooled off a bit, that don't mean you can go 'round in this heat bareheaded."

I was speechless. In self-defense, I was about to point toward Rayford and offer some kind of explanation when Papa Mike walked up with hat in hand. "Young man, you'd better keep up with your belongings."

Seeing Ollie Mae from afar was tantalizing and provided fodder for daydreaming, night dreaming, and other fantasies. Being near her, bringing her water, and having an up-close and personal view of that captivating body was intoxicating. Now, to have her speak directly and pointedly to me with care and consideration was … inexplicable. I doubted I would ever fall asleep that night.

Feeling relived when the young married group had quenched their thirsts, I wandered on over to the cluster where Mama and Billy were chopping. I felt good being an administrator, a water boy, something other than just another hoe hand. I was a role model for my little brother and I hoped a "big man" in my mama's eyes.

The junior youth, ages ten, eleven, and twelve, chopped cotton with their parents, or mostly their mothers. It was an arduous and tedious task to chop grass and weeds and save the cotton. Smaller children were notorious for chopping the cotton along with the grass.

It was common practice that children under age twelve weren't allowed to chop cotton on the first go-around when adultlike decisions had to be made in thinning three-inch-tall cotton plants from eight and ten plants down to three and four. The split-second decisions could mean the difference between a bumper crop and a sparse crop.

Cotton was chopped three times intensely, with a fourth time as an option, depending on the rain. The choppings were spaced at two, four, and six weeks when feasible. Heavy rains could unweave the rotation and wreak havoc.

I could tell by her mannerisms and the look she gave me that Mama was proud of my part in the storm-splitting incident. Later that evening, I would hear younger brother Billy say how she had doted. "That's not just any water boy; that's my boy with that ax." Little did she know that I was determined make her proud of me in my lifetime. I was determined to get her out of the cotton fields. In fact, my prayer, my plan, my mission was to liberate all of them. There had to be a better way of making a living.

My mother had steadfastly and consistently responded to personal inquiries as to "Why are we poor? Why are we black? Why are we in Mississippi?" with "One day you will understand." Understand? Why would God, who is a just God, make some people poor, some people black, and place the lot of them in Mississippi cotton fields?

I wanted to talk with God. Later that night, when all was quiet and everybody was bedded down, I would speak with God. This had been going on since age nine, when I joined the church after being baptized in Big Creek.

The preacher said, "God is all-powerful, all wise, all-knowing, and a just God."

Why are we out here chopping cotton on a plantation? I didn't know the answer right then. My soul wouldn't rest until I found a reasonable and logical answer.

Mama sang in the church choir, standing in the front line next to the piano. One of her favorite songs was "We'll Understand It Better By and By." She could really stand and deliver that song! I was flabbergasted that I couldn't understand right away why we were born poor, black, and in Mississippi. Why couldn't we have been born rich, white, and in Memphis? Why? Why? Why?

Mama was saying we would understand it better by and by. I was wondering if and when we would ever understand the reason for our plight. Did that mean fortunes would change? Would we still be black? Would we still be in Mississippi?

The preacher had said on several occasions that as Christians, "We walk by faith, not by sight" (2 Corinthians 5:7). Therefore, I resolved to trudge straight ahead, believing I would gain understanding, believing that one day I would not only be proud but exceedingly glad that I was born poor, black, and in Mississippi. Surely God Almighty Himself didn't make a mistake. Surely there had to be a reason for our plight in life.

CHAPTER 3

In the Heat of the Day

Mrs. Sara Parsons was a pint-sized rifle of a woman. She always wore dresses with an apron. Omnipresent and just as obvious was her pouched bottom lip stuff. She and Mama Rosetta's group chopped furiously, always in a hurry. In the aftermath of the storm splitting, they were huddled together like wild geese, talking and chopping.

Ms. Parsons owned and operated a snack bar. A better description would be a sandwich shop. She made sandwiches out of anything available and sold them on Saturday night from her porch right behind the Juke Joint. She had a stash of paper cups in her apron pocket. These were the kind of cups whites used at drinking fountains—cone-shaped disposables. Ms. Parsons was ahead of her time. She recycled and reused a cup as long as it held water.

She was reaching her cup out now, impatiently waiting for it to be filled. "Boy, where is your manners?" Hearing the tone of her own voice and seeing the bewilderment on Mama Rosetta's face, she mellowed and said kindly, "Would you please poor an old lady a cool drink of water?"

Obedient and well-mannered as always, I filled her cup, waited while she swallowed, and refilled it upon signal.

Somehow, I was the pride and joy of Mama Rosetta. I helped her twin granddaughters, Sudie and Judy, paint her living room and hallway walls for Christmas. Once, she gave me a whole sweet potato pie as a token of her appreciation.

On Saturdays, I became paper boy and delivered the *Grit* newspaper to twenty-three regular customers spread out over four and a half miles.

On Sundays, I became assistant superintendent of Sunday school and youth camp.

Today I was the closest eyewitness to Dolph Rhodes splitting the storm. They all wanted to ask, but protocol said if Mama Rosetta didn't ask, nobody should.

Mamie Lyons didn't quite understand protocol. She chopped to the music of a different drummer. Seizing the moment, she popped the question: "Did Dolph split that storm? What happened?"

Sheepishly, I looked up, and all eight pairs of eyes were looking my way.

Speaking to adults in church or Sunday school was different. I could always expect a chorus of amens, uh-huhs, well-wells, and the like—all positive reinforcements.

Here, this was a conversation with grown-ups, and I was the chief spokesperson.

"Mr. Dolph raised that ax, lightning flashed, and …" I didn't know whether they wanted the truth, the facts, or a cover-up. Adolph was an acknowledged sinner. He ran a gambling house. He was shacking with a woman. He had fathered three children outside holy matrimony. He didn't go to church for funerals or weddings, let alone regular service.

Yet, like Moses parting the Red Sea, he had split a storm. Or did he?

What was I to do? Conjuring up wisdom beyond my years, I lied through my teeth.

"The lightning hurt my eyes, and I shut 'em. When I opened them back up, the ax was in the ground, and the storm was parting just like that." I had put the bucket on the ground and spread my hands wide apart. "Didn't y'all see it?" My voice tailed off as I realized lying was a big mistake. Children are not to put grown-ups on the spot by forcing them to own up to something they don't want to tell or put in words.

Hurriedly, I lied again, further giving them a way out. "The lightning flashing musta hurt y'all's eyes too, didn't it? We may never know what really happened."

Mamie Lyons said, "I saw Dolph split the wind. The old folks used to tell us about it, but I never seed it 'fore today."

A stony silence fell over the old folks. Only the sounds of eight hoes chopping could be heard.

Then out of the blue came Papa Mike's booming voice from atop the truck's running board. "Here we go! Head 'em up! Dinnertime."

Whew! Saved again! I related the announcement: "Time to go! Dinnertime."

It was a motley crew that huddled onto the flatbed truck with wooden panels. Mama Rosetta rode up in the cab with Papa Mike. Mr. Parsons stood on the running board next to Mama Rosetta. The rest huddled on the back in their same clusters. The older group had priority and stood in the corners on each side closest to the truck's cab. Small children sat in the middle on the floor. Married people also had the middle, and teenagers took up space near the rear.

Dolph Rhodes was always the last to climb the moveable stepladder and sit down, with legs dangling over the back ledge. He pulled up the ladder and in a gruff voice yelled, "Here we go."

Everybody was looking at Dolph Rhodes, but not one peep came out about what he'd done. That is, until the truck stopped at the general store and Cupcake was descending the steps held by Dolph Rhodes.

"Mr. Dolph, I really appreciate what you did. That storm could have ruined my hair."

She peeled off her scarf as she spoke, revealing jet-black pressed locks, neat as a pin.

She looked at me and winked, then smiled and whispered, "See you this afternoon?"

Before I could attempt to answer, I whiffed the telltale aroma emitting from Ollie Mae as she descended the steps backward with that exogenic derriere bringing gasps from the cripples on the store porch.

Feeling the need to be protective, I moved to that side of the steps to shield her body from their view with my thin carcass. It was futile.

Ollie Mae loved to show off. Walking in front of men and in full view of envious women brought out the imp in her. She strutted her stuff.

The old men on the porch were too old, too crippled, or otherwise unable to perform farm work. Tractor driving required physical toughness and mental alertness. Cotton chopping was the graveyard for many tractor drivers. The store porch was the place for the totally incapacitated.

Dinnertime at the lunch hour is not a contradiction. Women folk began cooking around four thirty in the morning. Men and boys chopped the firewood before nightfall or before dawn for the stoves and often made the fire. Women cooked. Period.

During good times, there was a light breakfast of biscuits, rice, gravy, eggs, and sausage—milk maybe, juice hardly ever. During bad times, there were biscuits and molasses.

Cotton choppers worked from 6:00 a.m. to 11:00 a.m., followed by two hours for lunch, and then back to work until 6:00 p.m. This afforded women the time to fix dinner for their tractor-driving menfolk. Tractor drivers worked from 7:00 a.m. to 12:00 p.m., with an hour for lunch, and then 1:00 p.m. to 7:00 p.m.

Lunch was corn bread, peas or beans, ham hocks, grape Kool-Aid, and watermelon for dessert. Everybody always ate heartily, unless ill. They had to, in order to hold up under the challenging physical labor. A nap after lunch was an added blessing.

WDIA radio station 1070 in Memphis was the choice address on the AM dial. From eleven to noon was a gospel train featuring Ford Nelson. But at noon, it was time for the blues with Bob "Honeymoon" Garner. It seemed all right to listen to the blues once you heard some gospel. I didn't go home for lunch this time. Instead, I sat on the porch of the general store with the old-timers. I wanted to ask them something.

"Do y'all believe God only works through Christians, or does he work through sinners too?"

Peg-legged Joe Brown spoke right up. "God can work through anything, anybody. God is God. Why you ask?"

"Well," I said, "if a big storm was a coming, 'bout to blow away women and chilluns, and there were a whole lot of Christians standing there and a sinner or two there too, who God would pick to save everybody?"

Old Man Parker, a church deacon, felt the need to defend his turf. He said, "Well, you see, Joe is right. God does what he want to do, but he would pick his own to lead the unsaved. You see, boy, the blind can't lead the blind."

I wanted to tell them about Dolph Rhodes, but I couldn't afford to make grown-ups eat crow. I prodded further, "What you think, Mr. Paw-Paw?"

Everybody on the plantation knew Paw-Paw Davis was seeing a doctor about a heart problem. He was expected to return to rigorous hard labor in a week or two. I knew full well that he didn't like being part of the village cripples and that my line of questioning was annoying him to no end.

"Boy, what's in your head? Them 'fessors at school must be messing you up. Everybody knows God uses God-fearing men to save his people. Look at Abraham. Look at Moses. Look at Joshua."

One-legged James laughed. "Maybe we'd better demote you, bring you down a notch from young people catechizer. You been drinking?" Taken aback, I was somehow pleasantly surprised yet really amazed that Peg-Legged Joe Brown knew that I was the young people's catechizer in Sunday school. That is, after the various classes had finished their lessons and reassembled for reports, a deacon gave the adults an overview of what had been taught, and then the representative of the young people did likewise. I had been chosen the Sunday after my fourteenth birthday to represent the young people.

Papa Mike and the plantation foreman, Farley Bains, were walking from the office toward the general store. They'd walk a few steps, stop, talk, walk, stop, and talk. Mr. Bains seemed troubled, then elated, then laughing.

"Boys, have you heard? That big storm this morning bypassed Papa Mike and my cotton choppers. They didn't get a drop of rain and chopped all morning. We must be living right. Folks on Mark Hamm had a flood. They might not get back to plowing and chopping until next week."

A chorus of "That's so" and "The Lord works in mysterious ways" followed. I looked at Papa Mike's stoic expression. Papa Mike was not about to mention storm splitting and the sinner Dolph Rhodes.

This was no place for me. I grabbed my straw hat and, waving goodbye, broke out in a trot for the mile home. It felt good half-running—not like the all-out effort to get the ax for you-know-who but running just the same.

Middle ways between the general store and home, I had to pass the home of Dolph Rhodes. He was sitting on the porch, artfully peeling a green pear fresh from his backyard. Miss Cassie was undoubtedly preparing dinner. The children were pouring water in a furrow in the ground for the hogs, in a cut-out fifty-five-gallon can for the cow, and in partially buried gallon buckets for the chicken. It was steamy as the sun bore down. Farm animals needed water in the sweltering heat.

Dolph Rhodes's dark glasses were not a fashion statement. Light, especially bright sunlight, hurt albinos' eyes. Dolph Rhodes was half-reclining in the shade on his porch with the noonday sun glaring down from the clear sky after the storm. His dog, Fetch, started to bark.

I had an inherent aversion to dogs. It would be a misnomer to call it fear.

Aversion is the word. I would rebuke dogs with a verbal barrage. I did so this time. "Fetch, go hunt a rabbit and leave me alone. I am just a water boy!"

"Hey, Water Boy! That's you? Come heah a minute. I'll let you go. Just a minute of your time." Dolph Rhodes hailed me from the shade of his porch.

Obedient and polite to grown-ups, I coasted to the center, then leaped across the ditch into the gravel road, crossed over the plank walk by the mailbox, and walked briskly up to the porch. "Yes, sir, Mr. Dolph? Here I am."

"Sit down, boy. Let me holler at you about something." Dolph Rhodes was picking his words, slowly getting around to the real question.

"Boy, when I had you to run over to Eddie's house and fetch his ax, what did you think?"

"Mr. Dolph, I thought you wanted that ax real urgent-like. So I ran as fast as I could and got it."

"You sure did. But what did you figure I was gonna do with it, kill a snake?"

It was a trap. I looked around, and Miss Cassie was standing just inside the screen door, her white apron glistening against the background of a gray polka-dot dress. She said matter-of-factly, "Dinner is ready."

Dolph Rhodes dismissed her with a wave of his hand, without the benefit of a glance. She sauntered back to the kitchen and loudly summoned her three children to the table.

"Frankly, to tell the truth," Dolph Rhodes said, "I didn't know what I was about to do. Something just told me to tell you to get me that ax." He looked humbled, more like joyful, as he slumped on the porch bench—hands together, fingers tapping fingers, bottom lip drooped, dark glasses, coveralls, and a red handkerchief in the back pocket.

He turned in my direction, and I instinctively dropped my head, looked at the knotted pine floorboards, and said, "You split that storm. God worked through you. I felt it."

Dolph Rhodes froze like a marble statue in a park. Pigeons would have mistaken him for the real McCoy. He moved his lips, but no sound came out. He dropped his head a moment. Then he pointed his finger and said. "You tell Mama Rosetta God loves me too! Just 'cause I ain't perfect don't mean I ain't worthy. I am not God's stepchild!"

By this time, I was most uncomfortable with this man-to-man conversation. Like almost all children, I looked up to all grown people but especially the gruff and distant, like Mr. Dolph. I didn't know what to say, but my body knew what to do. I turned tail and started to move back to the plank walk by the mailbox. Polite and courteous as ever, I said respectfully as I left, "Yes, sir, Mr. Dolph, I will sure tell her."

I hurried home to where Mama would have some roasting ears, black-eyed peas, pork loins, corn bread, and presweetened grape Kool-Aid. I was wondering why our family preferred grape jelly, grape Kool-Aid, and just plain old grapes. Maybe it was the color purple, the color of royalty. Somehow, everything we liked as a family was the color purple.

At a quarter to one, right on schedule, Papa Mike backed the carrier truck out of his drive way and began making stops. As chairman of both the trustee board and deacon board, he was the head black religious man who actually lived in the community.

The church pastor commuted from Osceola, Arkansas, and regular service was only one Sunday, the fourth Sunday per month. Papa Mike was the man church members turned to for leadership, decisions, and just about everything else during the four to five weeks between pastoral Sundays. He was never paid. He never complained.

Why then, I wondered, didn't God use Papa Mike to work a miracle of storm splitting? Was he being punished for having committed something surreptitiously? Imagining Papa Mike committing sins and having thought of the word *surreptitiously* made me smile. I had stumbled upon it in class while looking for synonyms for secretively.

But why had God chosen Papa Mike's second-in-command in the cotton field to split the storm? Wasn't he a self-avowed sinful hoe filer? And didn't he have the lowly third-in-command, a mere water boy, fetch the ax?

Papa Mike the overseer had been overlooked while God used a sinner and a boy to work a miracle. Something was wrong with that picture. Something was mighty wrong. Or was it?

The carrier truck rolled to a stop on the turn road affronting the greenest hundred acres of four-week-old cotton a plantation owner would want to see. Plantation life, the societal structure based on race, always bothered me. Whites at the top regardless of age, gender, and physical attributes. Coloreds at the bottom in spite of talents, beauty, and brains.

There was something forebodingly sinister about that beautiful green expanse of cotton. Looking at it artistically, it was nature in all its glory. From a field hand's perspective, it was an albatross, a chain, a serpentine barbed wire fence. What was life like without cotton fields? I needed to know. Indeed, I would find out by and by.

At Sunday school every Sunday, James Randolph, husband to Katie Randolph, said proudly that the children were the future. Here were ten-, eleven-, and twelve-year-olds serving apprenticeship under the watchful eyes of their parents. Apprenticeships to become cotton choppers! This was their future!

What a messed-up world. Children tied to the land like medieval serfs, while God was using a nearsighted albino sinner to work a miracle.

A cotton chopper never resumed chopping in the same spot they left off at lunch. They started at the opposite end, with everybody hoping they would get one of the short rows started by Mama Rosetta's group. Papa Mike always assigned the shortest row to me, the water boy, just in case it got hot enough for water before the row was finished. All hoe hands understood and appreciated that. Usually, they joyfully helped Papa Mike identify the shortest row.

Cupcake knew that. She maneuvered and got the next to the shortest row. She wanted to be next to me. During lunch, she had put on a khaki shirt, lipstick, eyelash liner, starched blue jeans, and a straw hat with a drawstring. The scarf was missing. She was a thirteen-year-old with a bullet. She wanted the water boy.

During those days, I was just growing out of a childhood respiratory condition where breathing through my mouth was more easily done than through clogged nostrils. True, I had smelled the fragrance emitting from Ollie Mae that morning. Something about perfume led to stuffiness of my nostrils. But that was following my breathtaking dash to fetch the ax for Dolph Rhodes to split the storm. My air passageways had been blown wide open. Strange—at school, the boys and girls would say about having a crush on one another, "Nose are open."

During lunch, perhaps an allergic reaction to pepper, my nose had become clogged.

Cupcake had no way of knowing this. Her body reeked of Parisian Woods perfume. She smelled good to everybody except me. The aroma was stifling. I started to sneeze but muffled it. My recourse was breathing through my mouth.

I chopped on the adjoining row from Cupcake. Occasionally, she carelessly and perhaps intentionally brushed against me. Undaunted, I was preoccupied with God, children, future, cotton chopping, and storm splitting by sinners. I chopped in silence as Cupcake softly sang Jerry Butler's recent hit song, "For Your Precious Love." That was par for the course, as plantation field hands, especially cotton choppers, sang some kind of song either by themselves or in a group. Whiling away the time while chopping was more than a notion. It was a necessity. Maybe singing to oneself was a precursor to wearing earphones and listening to iTunes on iPods.

Dolph Rhodes was filing hoes. As usual, he started on row one and worked back toward me, the water boy, on the last row. Mama Rosetta had row one. This was standard. She believed you couldn't lead from behind. As first lady of the choppers her husband supervised, she was going to be a role model.

She handed her hoe to Dolph Rhodes in exchange for his substitute while he sharpened her hoe blade. Surely during the dinner break, she and Papa Moses had avoided the subject of the storm. I knew from experience that they viewed the actions of a sinner in what could have been a coup d'état of the acknowledged church leader. There, I had done it again—used a big term like coup d'état. I had to be careful not to use noncolloquial words. I certainly never, ever wanted to alienate myself from less educated and uneducated neighbors.

I gleaned from the several cotton-chopping clusters that no one disliked Dolph Rhodes. It was simply that he represented the sin that was preached against in church and decried in Sunday school, prayer meetings, and revivals. Dolph Rhodes was a first-class sinner. Without exception, each cluster wondered why would God use him in front of all these people—and not the first family of the church and the cotton field.

Was it not Mama Rosetta who had declared at starting time this morning that indeed a storm was coming? Was it not she who had seen the ring around the moon the night before? Wasn't it her bold announcement that thunder heard before seven meant rain before eleven? The old storm had come shortly before ten o'clock, an hour before eleven.

"Here's your weapon, Mama Rosetta." It was Dolph Rhodes handing her trusted hoe.

"Thank you, Mr. Rhodes." We all heard her say it. Otherwise, we wouldn't have believed it. For years, she had called him only by his first name. Now she was saying, "Mr. Rhodes." Was this God speaking through her like some erstwhile hollow reed?

Her words were not lost on me. They were not lost on Dolph Rhodes either. He chuckled loud enough to be heard as he moved on to Miss Mamie. Upon exchanging hoes, she blurted, "My husband read in the Bible in the book of Numbers that God once made a mule talk."

Brother Luke Lyons said, "Yeah, God says he will make the rocks cry out."

Minnie Plunk chimed in. "He spoke to Moses through a burning bush."

"And don't forget—that snake spoke to Adam and Eve."

Everybody was talking loud enough for Mama Rosetta to hear. Their words were intended for her ears. Somehow during lunch, the older cluster had come to the conclusion that God works in mysterious ways, his wonders to perform. Dolph Rhodes was one of those mysterious ways.

"Water Boy! Water Boy! Let me wet my whistle 'fore I turn into a thistle." It was Old Man Tanner. In bygone times, perhaps in another life, he would have been a town crier. He could be heard for miles, let alone for acres.

Putting down the hoe and picking up the bucket was nothing but a thrill for me. I waved to Mr. Tanner, acknowledging his request, and was about to make my way to the truck to make the switch from hoe to water bucket when I felt a tug on my right shirtsleeve. It was Cupcake. She was crying softly. "Why you don't like me?"

Words wouldn't come. Feet wouldn't move. I just stood there looking for the first time into love-struck eyes. It was fascinating yet frightening. She was underage, a child in a woman's body. I was not quite fifteen, and she had recently turned thirteen.

"Water Boy, get the lead out!" That was the voice of Papa Mike. It was an order, not a request. I bolted for the truck to fill the water bucket. Something was happening ... What in the world was I going to do with a thirteen-year-old? My fifteen-year-old "girlfriend" lived two miles away, and I mostly saw her at school and church. Now, this thirteen-year-old locked inside a woman's body was pulling my chain. What's a fifteen-year-old boy to do?

CHAPTER 4

OLLIE MAE

Dolph Rhodes and I arrived at Ollie Mae's row at the same time. It was no accident. I wanted the calming chaperoning presence of the hoe filer when encountering the breathtaking presence of Ollie Mae.

It was a smart move. Ollie Mae and Mattie Lee spoke almost in unison. "Mr. Dolph, we saw what you did. You saved us from that storm."

Mattie Lee, always the jokester, added sheepishly, "If you weren't so old and ugly, I'd do something special for you." She and Ollie Mae laughed together like two sisters sharing an inside joke. I liked the idea of an extended hand slap above their heads. I wondered what my buddies and I would look like doing that. Was it a girlish thing? Could boys do it?

Dolph Rhodes smiled humbly and mumbled, "It was nothing. Something just made me do it. I didn't know what I was doing. I'd never done it before. Never seen it before either."

"My mom," said Mattie Lee, "told me at dinnertime that she usta hear about church folks splitting the wind all the time. Most of the time, it was a preacher or deacon."

Dolph Rhodes was obviously perturbed as he retorted, "Well, what that make me? A preacher or deacon?"

Ollie Mae gave him a playful pinch on the cheek. "You are my teacher-preacher, my darling deacon." She and Mattie Lee broke out in laughter over "darling deacon." Rayford gave his approval. Nobody wanted water. I just stood there looking out of the corner of my eye at Ollie Mae, wondering what my future wife was going to look like. Like Ollie Mae? Like Cupcake? Nah. Maybe she wasn't even born yet.

Mama wanted water. She had been working hard trying to help Billy with his grassy row. He would turn thirteen in August and be free to mingle with teen peers. This was his last go-around as an apprentice. Big and strong for his age, he could look and work beyond his years. But just after lunch, he sometimes became sluggish. The parents were still carefully watching him since he had suffered polio symptoms at the age of ten. This was one of those times. He said mournfully, "I am going to be water boy next year. You are going to have to drive a tractor." Billy was right. Once you got a driver's license, tractor driving was a promotion. Manhood was imminent. There it was again. Coming of age meant a promotion from cotton chopper to tractor driver. Still black. Still poor. Still in Mississippi.

"Beep, beep, beep." It was the shop foreman, Mr. Jake. He had parked on the turn road by the carrier truck.

"Water Boy, go see what Mr. Jake wants." It was that voice again, Papa Mike giving orders.

I took off for the red Chevrolet pickup truck in my customary trot. The military calls it double time. Horse handlers call it a canter.

Mr. Jake was the third-in-command of Gorman Farms, with primary responsibility for the repair shop and service department. He was friendly, helpful, and extremely at ease with blacks.

"Hey, Water Boy, how are you? Will you go tell Ollie Mae my missus wants her to pick some Polk salad? Tell Papa Mike to give her straight time."

"Yessuh, Mr. Jake. I sure will."

I turned and walked hurriedly in the direction of the young married cotton choppers cluster where Ollie Mae was working. *On second thought, I better get this cleared.* I turned abruptly, headed to Papa Mike, and told him what Mr. Jake wanted. Papa Mike nodded his approval, took out his time book, and made a notation. He then asked Cupcake to take Ollie Mae's row in the married cluster.

Cupcake, who had been sulking, mumbled something under her breath and exclaimed to no one in particular, "I am going to the married group. I may not be married, but I am sure nuff in love." She looked directly at me with that last statement.

That little girl is a disaster about to happen. Gathering myself, I walked over to the young married group with Cupcake and related Mr. Jake's request to Ollie Mae. That is, I looked at her shoes as I spoke. There was no way I could look in her eyes and certainly no way would I dare look at her lips, and heaven forbid her ...

No, I couldn't even bother to think about it.

Rayford had overheard the request from Mr. Jake. He seemed self-assured in his marriage, without a hint of a jealous bone in his body. He needn't be duped by a white man. I knew about what was going on. You'd have to be a fool not to. Papa Mike knew. Dolph Rhodes knew. Just about everybody in our close-knit community knew about Mr. Jake. A lot of people were in on the know. Mr. Jake, friendly Jake, loved black women. Every so often, he would come and get one out of the cotton field to "help the missus around the house" or, like in this instance, "get something for the missus." This was the first time he had picked Ollie Mae. In previous escapades, he had wanted Lillie. She had moved away, and now he was apparently looking for another "helper."

My outward demeanor remained calm, but I was churning inside. Admittedly, I had some kind of misguided, sinful crush on Ollie Mae. Ollie Mae was married. What in the world was a not-yet-fifteen-year-old water boy doing with a crush on a fully grown woman? Worse, why was I coveting my neighbor's wife? Didn't the Ten Commandments make that clear? Didn't one of the commandments say explicitly, "Thou shalt not covet thy neighbor's wife"?

Was it not David who coveted Bathsheba, wife of Uriah the Hittite (2 Samuel 11:1–27)?

"But the thing that David had done displeased Jehovah" (2 Samuel 11:27). Whew! This thing was complicated. Maybe through some miracle I would someway, somehow get Ollie Mae out of my mind.

The slogan on the billboards, on the radio, on TV, and in newspapers promoting the 1957 Chevrolet was "Sweet, Smooth, and Sassy." Ollie Mae was personification of a 1957 Bel Air Chevrolet. Ollie Mae was sweet, smooth, and sassy. Now, that vision of loveliness, Ollie Mae, was going to be with Mr. Jake. Did she know what was up? How would she act? What should I do? Should I tell her? These questions raced through my mind as I watched my beloved Ollie Mae sashay between the green cotton rows, bound for the red pickup truck and Mr. Jake.

The more I thought about it, the more furious I became. I looked over my shoulder to see what Rayford was doing. He was flirting with the thirteen-year-old Cupcake as if she had taken his wife's place. I thought, *If she was my wife, I would kill anybody who even thought about being with her.* Then I felt ashamed about my thoughts. Life can be so cruel.

Papa Mike was leaning on his hoe handle but otherwise standing straight as an arrow in his khaki pants, matching khaki shirt, and sweatband-stained Stetson. Deacon Mike was probably sulking about not being the storm splitter for the midmorning miracle. What was the big churchman going to do about this?

But what proof did I have? Was I another Chicken Little proclaiming the sky was falling? Crying wolf without a corpus delicti was not a good idea. What could be done?

Over the years, Mr. Jake had taken Lillie, Mattie Lee, and others with him. They bragged about their "housework" and how "quickly" they had managed to finish. They also got "straight" time and went home early.

Mama Rosetta yelled out, "Water Boy!" I knew full well she didn't want water, at least the kind from the well; she wanted juicy information. Obedient, prompt, and for spite even, I took her water. Her whole cluster suddenly felt athirst.

"Was that Mr. Jake? What does he want with that young married woman? Where's he taking her? What did Papa Mike say?"

With the diplomacy of a man on trial, under oath, I blurted out the whole truth and nothing but the truth: "Yes, ma'am, that's Mr. Jake. His missus wants Ollie Mae to pick her some Polk salad from around that cane break over yonder. Then come to the house and fix 'em for supper. Mr. Jake asked Papa Mike to give her straight time the rest of the day."

"Did she go willingly? Or did she say no at first? What did her husband say?"

"She went willingly. Her husband didn't say a word. He is back there flirting with that thirteen-year-old." I was surprised at myself for giving so much information, especially that last bit about Cupcake. She was messing with my mind. I was hurting inside. I wanted to hurt somebody else. Maybe telling the truth and letting it cut like a two-edge sword would ease my pain. Gosh, I had a crush on Ollie Mae.

"Shame, shame, shame." Mama Rosetta was shaking her head from side to side in an exaggerated fashion. She looked every bit the part of some wounded bull ready to charge a matador. She continued, "It looks like slavery time all over again when master comes hunting dark skin. Colored women sure see a hard time."

Minnie Plunk looked at Mama Rosetta and back at me. "Hush up, Rose. This young'un ain't got any business hearing you talk about *s-e-x*."

"You mean he don't know about the birds and the bees?" asked Miss Mamie.

Miss Dora asked for closure on the subject. "All y'all need to keep your mouth closed. We don't know what that man wants with that woman. 'Sides, both of them grown."

Dolph Rhodes stood up from sharpening Miss Mamie's hoe for the third time that day. "Tell y'all what. You call yourselves Christians. You ought to let the Lord work through you and put a stop to white men raping colored women. Y'all free. Nobody gonna hang y'all. You can do it."

"Water Boy, run down there to the corner of the cane break and see if they going to pick any Polk salad." Mama Rosetta was shaking and pointing.

My Lord, Mama Rosetta, I thought. *Haven't you heard of Emmett Till?* I was thinking hard about following her directive. *What about Papa Mike?*

She read my expression. "Boy, you do what I say. I'll handle Papa Mike. You heah me? Now, you go like I say, you heah?"

I took off running but then decided to walk briskly instead. My chore this time was to gather information about a rape. Rape sounded like a nice word to be a bad word. I had never spoken it aloud. Sex was a no-no in polite conversation, and boys never used the word rape. They did talk about "taking" or coaxing. Word from menfolk like Peg-Leg Brown was that good girls never said yes. They always said uh-huh when they meant yes and no when they meant no.

I could see the red Chevrolet truck with the matching red windshield sun visor and silver propane tank on the back. It was moving slowly, going east where the Polk salad plants grew wildly and freely in a clump of trees along the swamp-like cane break. The truck was out of the line of sight of the cotton choppers. Only I could see it. Pausing to collect myself and catch my breath, I wondered, *What in the world am I doing?* It was two years ago that Emmett Till had been found castrated and dead at the bottom of the Tallahatchie River. What on earth would happen if Mr. Jake saw a black boy following him and a colored woman in a pickup?"

Terrified, I froze. God had used a sinner to save a field full of cotton choppers from a violent storm. Could God help me save Ollie Mae? Did she need saving? Did she want to be saved? Either she didn't know what was taking place or she was a willing participant. Which was it? I didn't know. I simply couldn't decide.

Dolph Rhodes's words at the lunch hour came to me in a low whisper: "Frankly, I didn't know what I was going to do. I just let myself go."

There, I had it. I decided then and there to just let myself go. I scurried low to the ground between underbrush in the direction of the red Chevrolet pickup truck.

I was sweating profusely. My palms were wet. I had experienced this a few times before. Once when cornered by Old Man Wiley's bull, another when I had to slit the throat of a hog during a hog-killing session. This was scary. Worse, the nagging question was, What was I going to do?

The pickup truck had stopped safely out of sight of anyone passing on the main road or the turn road. Only I knew where the truck was and who was in it.

I dropped to all fours, crawling through the knee-high-tall cotton plants to the turn road, and then through the thicket toward the cane break. My fear of being detected took the back burner after what I saw next.

Snake!

"My God, my God, why hath thou forsaken me?" The words came automatically, like the spontaneous spewing of a geyser. The moccasin was gray and brown and on the stubble of a sawed-off tree trunk.

Goodness knows I feared snakes, dogs, and the inside of a coffin—in that order.

Something was wrong. This snake was abnormal. It had big whiskers? It was a moccasin all right. It was swallowing a rabbit headfirst. Those were hind legs sticking out of the snake's mouth. The rabbit was a done deal. The snake had the upper hand. But the rabbit had not died in vain. It left the snake helpless for the moment. It couldn't run. It couldn't fight. It was harmless until the rabbit passed through its jaws.

An inner voice told me to pick up the snake by its tail and just behind the jaws. I obeyed.

That coldblooded animal felt cool in the summer heat and in the palm of my sweaty hand. Amid my discomfort, I mustered enough courage to carry the snake toward the red Chevrolet pickup truck. I could see the driver's side door wide open. No heads were visible through the back window. My heart was beating wildly. I had a three-foot moccasin by the tail. I was approaching a white man and a black woman, probably about to "do it." I was a black boy intruding in the private life of grown folks. Worse, I was crossing the line into white folks' business.

"God help me." The words came naturally. So did the courage and the purpose. I could see Mr. Jake's naked backside, his pants below his knees beside the truck with his upper body and arms inside the truck. Ollie Mae must have been inside. I crept closer.

The snake was squirming but surprisingly not much. The rabbit was apparently an overdose. The snake's eyes were bigger than its belly. Make that its mouth.

I had no plan, but I knew instinctively what to do. I would creep up behind Mr. Jake and put the snake in his pants just below his knees. Then what? I couldn't think. I could only act while following that inner voice.

Aiming carefully and with the adeptness of ringing a horseshoe, the snake was hurled through the air and landed in the crotch of Mr. Jake's pants. In a flash, I was behind the truck. I heard Mr. Jake scream, "What the hell? My God, something got me, something got me!" Ooh, goddamn, it's a snake—it's a snake. Goddamn it. Goddamn, it's a snake! It's a snake. Oh, holy. Oh, my God!"

"What's wrong, Mr. Jake? What is it?"

"Where did it come from? What's wrong with it? Lord, have mercy."

I didn't dare move. In fact, I couldn't move. Paralysis set in as I was crouched just under the open tailgate. I could envision Mr. Jake looking around to see whether anybody else was in the vicinity.

Ollie Mae had become frightened and scrambled out of the passenger door. She was standing there with only a man's shirt. She reached back inside the truck and pulled out her blue denim pants. She was about to step in them when Mr. Jake fired his first two shots. He had regained enough composure to reach inside his glove box and retrieve a Smith and Wesson .38 handgun.

The snake was dead from the first volley, but in his rage, Mr. Jake fired twice more.

My heart was beating so fast I put both hands over my chest trying to quiet it. I was not sure about the shots. Were they meant for the snake? Me? Holy Moses! What had I done?

Mr. Jake must have put his clothes on. I couldn't tell, as I was still secluded under the rear of the truck.

Mr. Jake was talking fast. "Ollie Mae, start picking Polk salad. That's it—Polk salad."

Rayford, Carl, and Billy were the first to arrive on the shooting scene. Mable was next. Everybody else came in waves except Dolph Rhodes and Old Man Tanner.

I eased from under the cover of the truck and stood by Carl and my younger brother on the passenger side of the truck. Only Ollie Mae saw me emerge. She looked puzzled at first and then smiled knowingly. She nodded. I was too flustered to acknowledge it.

Mr. Jake was explaining to Rayford what happened. "I tell you—Ollie Mae was pulling the missus some of that fresh Polk salad when I saw this big fat moccasin catch this rabbit. I shot the thing before he could bother Ollie Mae."

Mr. Jake held the snake up by its tail in a triumphant manner. "Well, this is one you won't have to worry about anymore. He learned his lesson. The only good snake is a dead snake."

"All right, we had our fun. Let's get back to work. We have another two and a half hours to work. Let's go!" Papa Mike had arrived and as usual was a taskmaster. He was always focused, never distracted. The task at hand, whether work, family, or church, was a one-track-minded entity.

That's why Old Man Oscar had selected him years ago, just after World War II. He had held it ever since, chopping in spring and summer and picking in late summer and fall. Papa Mike was efficiency personified.

The hoe hands were back to work, still buzzing about the dead cottonmouth moccasin with the cottontail rabbit stuffed in his jaws. Ollie Mae had come back to finish the day chopping. Mr. Jake had suddenly released her from the duty assignment of "helping the missus," saying he was too shaken by the snake incident to drive home. He was going to sit there awhile and smoke a cigarette or two.

Ollie Mae let Cupcake keep her row with the married cluster, saying, "I am going to help the children, Papa Mike. They need me!" There was no objection.

I figured Ollie Mae wanted to avoid questions. There was no way the women with children were going to bring up any subject remotely related to the Polk salad escapade in front of the children. Ollie Mae knew that. Papa Mike knew that. I knew that. Everybody figured as much.

Rayford seemed oblivious to all the inquiring minds and unspoken questions. He was busy resuming his conversation with Cupcake, telling her how he was so often mistaken for his namesake, Ray Charles the singer.

CHAPTER 5

FORTY ACRES FOR A 1953 MERCURY

Jessie Blue was married and a landowner, farmer, barber, church usher, and leading citizen of the black community. One catch: he and his wife, who could not drive, had no children, and they were in their seventies. Perhaps, feeling the twinges of old age ailments steadily creeping into his world, Jessie Blue made a deal with plantation bookkeeper Jimmy Keyes: the white man would sign a bill of sale, selling a maroon 1953 Mercury for the deed to the black man's forty acres upon the latter's demise. Meanwhile, the black man could live on the land, till the soil, and go on doing what he had always done until death, while owning the 1953 Mercury.

The black community cried foul, foolish, and some other F words. Cotton choppers had a field day on the transaction. Each group of choppers had a different perspective, but they all talked about it.

As would be expected, Mama Rosetta and her entire group of aging choppers were absolutely against it. "Crazy man. He could have given that land to the church. What was wrong with his old Chevy?"

"Suppose he dies first? Then his wife is going to be homeless."

"I always figured Jessie to have better sense than that. Wait till I see him at church. I am going to give him a piece of my mind. He knows better than to give his land to the man. He could have sold it to the pastor or some other black folks."

I listened intently and wondered what the fuss was all about. The black man owned the land but wanted to spend the rest of his days living on that land and enjoying a four-year-old Mercury automobile.

Worried that my thinking was different from that of the elderly group, I made my way over to where my mother was chopping. Offering water as I approached, the thought occurred as to how a conversation about the car and land could be jumpstarted.

The question became moot as Old Man Tanner hollered out, "Lord, look a yonder. Here comes Jessie Blue!" The maroon Mercury was moving slowly along the gravel road from the direction of James and Maggie's house. Mr. Blue seldom drove more than thirty miles an hour. He savored each mile, each half mile, perhaps each quarter of a mile traveled in his maroon Mercury. As the powerful automobile moved along, a tiny wisp of a dirt cloud rose from the gravel and dirt road. Undoubtedly, Mr. Blue was making his daily trip to the general store. The car would pass along in front and then turn along the left side of the choppers. Choppers would get a panoramic view of the maroon Mercury.

Mama said quietly but with deep conviction, "Let the man enjoy himself. We all wish we could spend our last days in the lap of luxury. Maybe he is at peace and happy." Then she added a disclaimer: "'Lay not up for yourselves treasures upon earth, where moth and rust doth corrupt, and where thieves break through and steal. But lay up for yourselves treasures in heaven, where neither moth nor rust doth corrupt, and where thieves do not break through nor steal: For where your treasure is there will your heart be also'" (Matthew 6:19–21).

She wasn't through.

"'Judge not, that ye be not judged. For with what judgment ye judge, ye shall be judged: and with what measure ye mete, it shall be measured to you again. And why beholdest thou the mote that is in thy brother's eye, but considerest not the beam that is in thine own eye?'" (Matthew 7:1–3).

Mama was waxing biblically and spouting scriptures like an evangelist. There, I had done it again: thought in big words that I never uttered aloud. I wondered whether a person's written vocabulary and his spoken vocabulary would ever be on the same page.

Feeling ill at ease amid the outpouring of scriptures, I moved on to the group where Ollie Mae was chopping. The conversation about the car was full-blown. Mattie Lee was joking around that she wished she had known that Jessie Blue would give up his land just to feel good. "I could've had him laughing, giggling, coughing, spitting, and anything else. Course, the undertaker would have taken three days to get that smile of his dead face." The group was falling down with laughter.

I eased the water bucket over to Ollie Mae. She took the dipper and seized the moment to watch the maroon Mercury pass along the left side of the choppers. She said just above a whisper, "I am going to enjoy riding in that air-conditioned Mercury."

I figured women judged men primarily by wealth and status. Broke men and especially underemployed boys didn't stand a chance. Ollie Mae was only talking about riding in air-conditioned comfort. Maybe, she didn't see the driver at all. I began to ponder just how long was it going to be before I had a car of any kind, let alone one with refrigerated air inside.

Joker was holding court as usual: "Man, if I could get that fine car, I would give up eighty acres, two fat cows and a mule."

His sister interrupted his tirade with "Fool, don't you know if you had eighty acres, you could go to the bank and borrow $5,000 and buy yourself a Mercury, an old truck, and a few head of cattle?"

"But wouldn't you still have to pay for the Mercury? I would give up the land, drive the car, and die smiling … after I lived for another hundred years." The gang took upon the longevity aspects of the agreement.

"Yeah," Dimp said, "suppose Mr. Blue lives for another twenty-five or thirty years?"

Not meaning to pour water on the situation, I spoke for the first time: "Remember it ain't no sin to kill a black mockingbird. Mr. Jessie Blue is a black mockingbird. If he lives too long, he just might get a helping hand to glory."

CHAPTER 6

DEADLY CROP-DUSTING

The double-winged crop duster was making a wide, arching turn over the drainage break. Apparently, it had just taken off from the landing strip in front of the general store. I had always been intrigued by flying objects—from birds, to kites, to airplanes. I often wondered what it felt like to be up there, high above the ground, floating, sailing, soaring, and looking down. I vowed to one day soar above the ground and enjoy the view from above.

There were six planes anchored at the Garmon Farms landing strip: three double-winged crop duster planes, one single-winged crop duster plane, and two Piper passenger planes. This one was canary yellow, probably piloted by that foolish young white man, Mr. Bo Dukes. He had been dishonorably discharged from the navy but somehow had used the GI Bill to become a pilot. Of the three double-winged crop dusters—red, yellow, and silver—he loved flying the yellow one. Extremely adventuresome, he loved taking chances like clipping the tops of pine trees, flying under power lines, and scaring the hell out of cotton choppers.

I looked up and saw the big yellow plane dive just after it cleared the tree line. I could scarcely believe my eyes. The pilot was dumping his load of insecticide. On us!

"My God, he is spraying our field." I was whispering to no one in particular. Then I was hollering to Papa Mike a stone's cast away. "Bo Dukes is spraying our field! Bo Dukes is spraying our field!"

By now, most of the hoe hands heard the familiar whine of the crop duster's engine. Fear gripped those in direct line of the plane. Four fields were end-on-end stretching one full mile. Each field was called a quadrant, as in quadrant one, quadrant two, quadrant three, and quadrant four. The choppers were working in quadrant three. The crop duster was spewing insecticide from an altitude of twelve feet in quadrant one, now quadrant two, and coming at a speed of eighty miles per hour directly at thirty-two choppers.

The liquid spray covered about twenty-four rows on each pass of a crop duster. The plane itself spanned twelve rows. The rotating front propeller was bone-chillingly frightful. The wingspan was deadly. The drenching with insecticide was dreadful. Pandemonium broke loose. Those in Mama Rosetta's group tried to move by going laterally. Too slow. They fell to the ground. The married cluster and the cluster of mothers with children were directly in the line of flight. All they could do was fall flat to the ground, mothers screaming at children, "Get down! Get down! Cover your head!" The teenagers were to the far side. Terrified, they ran and crawled further from the path of the crop duster.

Papa Mike and Dolph Rhodes had been standing on the turn road chuckling about the Polk salad or whatever when they heard me yelling and the crop duster humming. They were directly in its path. Instinctively, they fell to the ground, Papa Mike begging, "Have mercy, Lord."

And Dolph Rhodes saying, "Damn, cracker, you trying to kill us!"

I was at the carrier truck out of danger and scared crazy for Mama, brother Billy, sister Dimp, and the rest. I muttered, "God save us! God save us!"

The plane skimmed over the bodies sprawled on the ground, writhing with fear and now drenched with insecticide.

I could see the pilot's face partially covered with goggles but bareheaded with Elvis-styled locks blowing in the wind. It was Bo Dukes all right, and he was laughing.

The crop duster went on by, spraying quadrant four, and then spindled upward and began a wide turn to the right before leveling off, turning left, and …

"He's coming back! He's going back!" I yelled.

Frantic, I thought quickly. What if the truck was moved a hundred feet up the turn road in line with the choppers? The crop duster would have to alter its path or at least increase its altitude. I jumped behind the wheel, turned the switch on, patted the accelerator five times, and pressed the floor starter. The carrier truck came alive. I depressed the clutch, threw the floor shift into second gear, and the old Chevrolet carrier truck lurched forward.

Bo Dukes apparently couldn't see the hunkered-down choppers, but probably using the truck as a reference point, he brought the plane down about ten feet from the cab of the truck, which was out of line with the unseen choppers. His second flyover missed the group altogether.

I heard Papa Mike shout, "Here we go! Everybody, get to the truck! Right now!" I figured he'd seen enough for a whole long dry spell. A storm split by the biggest sinner in town. A snake with whiskers. And now a dang fool white man in a plane. What else could happen?"

Death.

Miss Lula wasn't moving. Her eyes were bucked, looking but not seeing. Her mouth was agape. "Lula, Lula, what wrong? Speak to me, Lula!" Miss Lucille was screaming in a shrill voice, which for her was hard to do considering the stash of snuff in her bottom lip.

I was torn in three directions: Was Papa Mike upset that I had put the truck in the path of the crop duster? That fool Bo Dukes was coming back a third time. And what in the world was wrong with Miss Lula?

The answers to the first and second questions came in rapid-fire order. Papa Mike was hollering, "Get out that truck, young fella! Who said you could drive my truck?" The crop duster had swung around but was now over behind Miss Mills's house. I could see a flag man waving a white flag at the end of quadrant one. That's where Bo Dukes was supposed to be, way over there.

Relieved, I jumped out of the truck and ran across the cotton rows to where six or seven people were gathered around Miss Lula.

She was dead. I hadn't seen a dead person before other than at a funeral. But I was thoroughly convinced that I was face-to-face with a warm corpse for the first time. A sinking feeling took a nosedive in the pit of my stomach. Death seemed so final, and death up close and personal was overwhelming. I ran back toward the truck where most insecticide-soaked choppers were gathering.

"She is dead, Mama. Miss Lula is dead."

It was four o'clock, two hours before quitting time.

I was running again. This time headed for the gravel road. A car was visible near the Barksdale Bridge, moving in the direction of the general store. Papa Mike was hollering orders even though they were already being carried out. "Water Boy, go hail that car and tell them to call a doctor or call the high sheriff. We got a dead woman out here."

I ran hard, just like that morning when I was going to fetch Mr. Etoy's ax for Dolph Rhodes. My chest started to burn in that now familiar way. I had to cover a quarter mile to intercept the approaching car. Luckily, the light blue roadster was moving at about a moderate forty-five miles per hour.

Wheezing, panting, and out of breath, I jumped the drainage ditch right on the gravel road, right in the pathway of the light blue roadster. I am sure my eyes were big from all the excitement. My shirt was open down the front, with only one button still intact. Loveable, amicable, everybody's friend, I must have presented a menacing sight to Mrs. Jeanette Keyes, wife of the plantation's bookkeeper. She was a housewife taking medication for a nervous disorder.

The sudden appearance of an arm-waving, ill-clad black male undoubtedly interrupted the serenity of her train of thought. I saw stark fear in her face. Jeanette Keyes panicked. She screamed and swerved to the right, running the roadster headlong into the three-foot drainage ditch. It stuck in the mud.

She was sobbing and screaming hysterically, "Don't touch me! Don't touch me!" I was terrified out of my wits. Fear came in waves. This crazy white woman thought I was trying to rape or rob her. *Emmett Till, God, and Emmett Till.* Thoughts raced through my mind. *Black boy, white woman. Mississippi. Oh, God.* I looked for help, a place to hide, a hole to crawl in, a way out. There was none.

I began to pray aloud, unabashedly, "Almighty, all-powerful God, please help me. I need help, Lord. Please, sir, have mercy." I believed in prayer. Not unusually, I would spend a rainy day in bed praying and meditating. The same was true of long, dark nights when sleep was elusive. Unquestionably, I knew the power of prayer. The answer to this prayer came when the red Chevrolet pickup truck turned onto the gravel road from the direction of the cane break. It was Mr. Jake. He had partially recovered from his drunken stupor following the moccasin snake incident. He was headed for the general store.

Mr. Jake had spent the last hour or so in prayerful meditation. As I understood things after the fact, good ol' Jake took the close encounter with the snake as some sort of divine sign. Now, I don't think it was a divine sign at all, 'cause I know exactly what went on. But ol' Jake? Not so much! He knew that seducing black women was wrong. They couldn't fathom saying no to his advances. Fear of white reprisals was omnipresent in all colored-white confrontations where colored people were adverse to white whims.

I can imagine Mr. Jake had promised himself and Almighty God that he was never, ever going to do it again. Surely, he took a deep, deep drink of the Hiram Walker Ten High Scotch Whisky he had hidden behind the seat. The scotch was for his boss, who always asked for a drink whenever he rode as a passenger in the red pickup. Mr. Jake, to my knowledge, didn't drink. That is, until today. That snake had all but scared him to death.

The noise of the crop duster must have gotten Mr. Jake's attention. He would later disclose apologetically that he had given specific instruction for Bo Dukes to spray the south side of Noah Road on the McCraney place. In fact, that's where he had dropped the two flag boys off, before coming to get Ollie Mae. God, she looked delicious!

I can imagine Mr. Jake kept asking, "Now, why on the earth was the crop duster spraying over near the choppers?"

My imagination was running rampant. Somehow I was having a mind melt with Mr. Jake. I could just hear him saying, "Near, my foot! That fool was spraying my choppers!" Surely Mr. Jake was upset. He probably reached for his keys, finding they weren't there. I could see and hear him vividly in my extrasensory perception: "Where are my keys?" He looked on the ground beside the truck. There was only the twitching carcass of the bullet-riddled cottonmouth moccasin. He searched his pockets. He looked behind the seat where sweet Ollie Mae had been. *God, she was one delectable dish. If only …* He remembered his promise to God to repent. Exasperated with the idiotic antics of Bo Dukes and the crop duster and frustrated at not finding his keys, he kicked the snake in disgust. The keys had been on the ground under the snake. No way I knew for certain these things were happening, but out-of-body experiences were not uncommon. In fact, they were too often, too vivid, and frequently downright frightening.

I shook my head violently from side to side, trying to rid my mind of Mr. Jake, the snake, and the red pickup. No such luck. I could visualize Mr. Jake grabbing his keys off the ground where the snake had shielded them from view, jumping into the truck, and heading to the gravel road. I could hear him muttering, "I am going to fire Bo Dukes on the spot. That redneck was out of his mind. He could kill somebody. He could harm a hair on the head of that round-bottom Ollie Mae. Oh, man, I have got to get that big-butt woman out of my system."

Mr. Jake came into my view just as Mrs. Keyes's car turned abruptly and slammed into the ditch. He was no longer in my mind but in my sight. I hoped beyond hope that he recognized me standing in the middle of the gravel road. Something wasn't quite right. Despite his love for colored women, Mr. Jake was a fair and level-headed man. He would know instantly that I, no other boy, colored or white, would dare cross paths purposely with Jeanette Keyes. Her grits weren't in the middle of her plate. She was to be avoided at all costs.

"Mr. Jake! Miss Lula done fell dead. Miss Keyes done run in the ditch. What's we to do?" There it was again. When under pressure, I had a tendency to lapse into colored dialect. Maybe it was self-defense.

Maybe it was self-survival. Right now, I was double scared, triple scared. Did Mr. Jake know where the snake came from?

Mr. Jake was in his element. He was adept at problem-solving and handling nonpersonal crises. "All right, calm down, Water Boy. Let's get Miss Keyes situated first."

Seeing Mr. Jake, Miss Keyes fell into a rapid-fire tirade: "Jake, that boy jumped out in the road trying to attack me. Shoot him! Kill him! Do something!"

"Shhh, shhh. Hush now, Miss Keyes. He was trying to get help. He didn't mean you no harm. A colored woman done fell dead out there.

"Miss Keyes, you done already run one of Cora's boys away from home. We just can't let you do that again, can we? You know that boy weren't about to bother you. Now quiet down, you hear?" Mr. Jake was venting.

Looking back on that eventful year of 1957, I knew even then at age fourteen that things were never going to be the same. Not for me. Not for us. Not for Mr. Jake. He had a different perspective I didn't quite get at the time, but I figured it was about right just the same. I figured he wanted what I did, and that was for the white folk around our neck of the woods to stop messing with the black folk. Slavery was done and gone, but its spirit still seemed alive and well. And I hated that. Somehow, I got the idea that Mr. Jake was going to do his part in his own way.

Miss Keyes was obviously perturbed by Mr. Jake's tone of voice but calmed down nonetheless. She and her circle of white lady friends looked down on Mr. Jake as "poor, uneducated white trash." I was guessing she could add the final nail in his coffin: "Nigger lover." At the bridge club or whatever club meeting, she had plenty to whisper about between deals. She had an ace up her sleeve, and she was more than likely going to use it.

At my young age, I knew that surely Mr. Jake realized the backlash from any pro-colored stance by a white man. This was not just a pro-colored stance; it was a righteous stance. Something within him suddenly seemed to want to do the right thing.

Feeling relieved is an understatement. God had answered my prayer and sent Mr. Jake. I was feeling so appreciative—yet guilty about the snake at the same time. Mr. Jake's words were soothing to my mind, though Miss Keyes had yet to digest the situation and acquit me of any attempted crime. She was still ranting.

"All colored boys think about is us white women. We can't sleep, can't eat, can't live in peace 'cause of them." Looking right at me, she said, "Get yourself one of them foul-smelling nappy-headed colored girls. Let us alone. We don't want you. White folks don't even want to touch colored folks."

"Come now. Calm down, Miss Keyes," Mr. Jake pleaded. "He wasn't trying to bother you. He was trying to get help.

"Boy," Mr. Jake said, "did that fool Bo Dukes hit that woman? Did he kill her with the airplane?"

"No, sir, Mr. Jake. The plane scared her. She just fell dead. A heart attack or something. Must have scared her to death!" I was telling it as I figured it.

Mr. Jake got a chain from the bed of the red pickup and was tying it to his front bumper. He motioned for me to put the tow hook end of the chain under the rear bumper of the roadster. I obliged. Miss Keyes was still standing in the road fuming but obviously better, or close to understanding the situation. I refused to look her way but obediently followed Mr. Jake's directive and eased behind the wheel of the roadster. I put one foot on the brake, one on the accelerator, slipped the gear in reverse, and revved the engine.

The red pickup backed up, stretching the chain taut, and with minimum effort pulled the roadster from the three-foot-deep drainage ditch back onto the gravel road.

"Boy, apologize to Miss Keyes. Promise to clean up her car or something," Mr. Jake said.

Timid. Tired-tongued. Terrified. I heard a small voice come from my mouth: "I am sorry I spooked you. I will wash your car this evening at six o'clock, soon as quitting time." I was not sucking up. I was sincere. Mama always said that which comes from the heart goes to the heart. My words must have touched this seemingly heartless woman. Miss

Keyes nodded in acknowledgment. She got into her roadster and quietly drove off.

Mr. Jake, speaking in even, authoritative tones, said, "Hop on the running board, Water Boy. Let's go see about that dead woman." It wasn't proper for colored males to ride inside the cab with a white boss. Most of the time, colored boys and men rode on the back of the truck. This time, Mr. Jake was giving me a promotion to the front side of the truck. I felt important. I felt good. He drove the red Chevrolet pickup right out to the spot where Miss Lula lay. He ran over cotton roads with obvious reckless abandonment. He didn't demonstrate any care about the cotton plants. He just headed for the huddle of cotton choppers around the body of Miss Lula.

There was Ollie Mae, slightly off to the side, leaning on her hoe handle with her already attention-grabbing backside more obvious. Riding on the running board on the passenger side of the truck, pretending to look straight ahead, I had to take a look at Ollie Mae as we drew near. I wondered to myself whether Mr. Jake was eyeing the same spectacle.

After checking for vital signs, Mr. Jake said, "She's dead. Let's put her on the back of the truck and take her home." I was thinking that even a dead colored woman couldn't ride upfront.

Papa Mike spoke up in a take-charge voice. "Mama Rosetta, you and the two mothers of the church, Miss Parsons and Miss Katie Randolph, go on over to Miss Lula's house on Mr. Jake's truck.

"The rest of y'all, get on the carrier truck. We're going home. There's been too much excitement for one day. We will get a new start early in the morning. Don't worry about your pay." Papa Mike was in charge. Everybody obeyed.

"You two, come over here." Papa Mike motioned for Dolph Rhodes and me to join him a little ways from where cotton choppers were boarding the truck.

He looked tired, almost defeated, but was unbowed, tall, and straight as ever. He took out a starched and ironed white handkerchief (Mama Rosetta washed and ironed every Saturday morning) and blew his nose in a loud, exaggerated fashion. Dolph Rhodes stood his Coca-Cola bottle crate on its long side and sat on it. He was in no hurry. I was emotionally drained and needed something to lean on. Trouble being, there was nothing. I just stood military-style parade rest.

"We have had more excitement in this one week than we had altogether for the last ten years. Chances are things will settle down tomorrow and be normal." Papa Mike was talking to the old man and the young man, but his eyes were watching the carrier truck. He continued, "I don't know why God chose to work through the two of you, but I am glad that he used somebody to do his will. We needed the Lord two or three times over the last several days."

Papa Mike in his own way was saying thank you. He was also admitting to Dolph Rhodes that he harbored no ill will for God having worked through a sinner. He was telling me thanks for my quick wit in helping with problems.

"Water Boy, will you help me up the steps, please, sir?" It was Cupcake. She was looking at me and pretending she had difficulty mounting the five rungs on the stepladder at the back of the carrier track. Mind you, older ladies and others had already ascended the steps and were in their usual places. Cupcake wanted attention. My attention.

I looked at Papa Mike for a dismissal from our caucus. His expression had finality. The briefing was over. The three of us walked in the direction of the carrier truck. Walking faster than the old guys, I reached out and held Cupcake's left elbow as she did her best Scarlet O'Hara impersonation in gliding up the steps.

Dolph Rhodes was whistling softly to mask his wheezing. Almost always out of breath, he turned would-be wheezes into softly whistled tunes. He walked up the steps behind me, pulled the ladder up behind himself, and sat down flat on the truck bed, legs hanging off the back. He was whistling a new song this time, "'Nobody knows the trouble I've seen. Nobody knows my sorrow ... Nobody but Jesus." Was Dolph Rhodes having a conversion?

"Thanks," Ollie Mae whispered. She was speaking to me for the first time since the snake incident. It was only one word, and it was said so discreetly no one else heard it amid the din of high-charged conversation about quitting early. I heard it. Goose bumps broke out like hives. My heart was palpitating at the thought that Ollie Mae, magnificent Ollie Mae, was talking at me and saying a word meant only for me! If only there was some kind of way to preserve this moment. I felt special. I felt important. I felt appreciated. Ollie Mae had said, "Thanks." Better yet, she had spoken directly, personally, privately, only to me! But, commandment ten of the Ten Commandments says, "Thou shalt not covet thy neighbor's wife." Was I coveting? My thoughts came back to the business at hand. If she was saying thanks, that meant she was unwilling to accommodate Mr. Jake. Didn't it? I was probing myself for that answer. Of course, she was an innocent victim of sexual harassment, sexual battery, sexual molestation, attempted rape. She was saying thanks to me, her rescuer, her knight without shining armor. I felt good all over. I mustered a smile while peering straight ahead, looking at the back of Dolph Rhodes's head. Feeling guilty, I then looked around to see if anyone had noticed my private moment with Ollie Mae.

Cupcake was looking at me with dreamy eyes, and as far as I could tell, only she could see that smile flitting across my face. Evidently, she thought my smile was for her; she pretended to lose her balance and slid three feet across two other choppers to land against my supportive arm.

"You coming to our house to watch television tonight?"

Embarrassed at the slight commotion, I thought for a moment and then replied, "I think I will."

CHAPTER 7

WATCHING TELEVISION

We didn't have a television set in our household. Very few people, white or colored, had TV sets on our plantation. Having one of the first television sets among some three hundred black families makes a household the favorite destination. Papa Mike and Mama Rosetta had one. So did the Harvey Green family. Word was also that John and Katie Randolph had a television. But those didn't matter. Having a TV set and welcoming a hoard of community people into your home are two different things. Yet that is exactly what Cupcake's parents, Elder and Sister Roy Baker, did on a nightly basis. They even went so far as to establish a weekday curfew of 9:00 p.m. and weekend curfew of 10:00 p.m. Their generosity and high rate of tolerance for having their neighbors over so often bordered on sainthood.

The Bakers had a black-and-white TV with what must have been a twenty-inch screen. Every night after work, six thirty to nine o'clock, dusty, often barefooted field hands and some grown-up tractor drivers crowded into the Bakers' largest room, which held two beds, maybe a sleeping sofa, and perhaps six chairs. Virtually no black Delta family had a stand-alone living room or family room in those days. Every room except the kitchen was a bedroom, although some hard-pressed families had a bed in the kitchen near the cooking stove.

Viewers sat on the floor, on each other, and just about everywhere in the Bakers' TV room. Out of courtesy, most guests deferred and gave the bed and sofa to the four children in the host family. The parents were usually in an adjoining room reading the Bible or doing something else. Sister Baker was nearly bedridden with a debilitating illness. Occasionally, Elder Baker would poke his head in to quiet down exuberant viewers. Sister Baker was almost always reticent and demurring. She was friendly, cordial, and polite but had little to do with the assemblage of community persons. At best, she would say, "Enjoy yourselves. Y'all come back again anytime."

I remember that the oldest Baker child was a nineteen-year-old boy who was trying to establish his own homestead in a nearby location. He was in and out of the house and gone for days at a time. The three daughters, ages seventeen, fifteen, and thirteen, were as different from one another as could be. The older girl, Dee Dee, was full of both comedy and mischief. She loved to play with words and would talk over the telecast. It was she who would start a loud outburst and cause Elder Baker to occasionally enter the room to issue a warning.

The middle girl, Cookie, tended to be shy and reserved but had that really nice snicker when someone or something tripped her tickle button. Cupcake, the baby girl, was pure jailbait. Her body was fully developed ahead of schedule. She stood barely above five feet, but outside of being a little plump, she was well proportioned from head to toe. Like a child with a new toy, she flaunted her proportioned body by dressing up to watch TV. Boys and men alike gave her more than passing attention. But Elder Baker was more than respected. He was also feared. Nobody dared get out of line with his little girl.

On the fateful week of the storm splitting, I broke away from the questioning at the general store just before seven o'clock and walked the hundred yards to the Bakers' to watch *The Lone Ranger*. I had not wanted to watch *Amos and Andy* at six thirty. Something just wasn't right with that display of tomfoolery. "The golden age of TV" had absolutely no blacks in positive role model telecasts. At that point, I had no idea if the future would bring about change.

In hindsight, I ought to have expected the grown-ups of the Baker household to be curious and question me about the storm-splitting episode. Somehow, my mind and full attention was dead set on hearing William Tell's Overture heralding the masked rider of the western plains. Knocking politely, I heard a voice say, "Come in." It was Elder Baker.

"Hey, Water Boy. I heard you had a busy, busy day the other day. Sit a spell and let me ask you something." I spoke respectful words of greeting to Sister Baker, who was friendly but quiet as usual. She was reclining in a large stuffed chair with feet elevated on a stool. Almost always, she was either sick or recovering from one illness or another.

Elder Baker was sitting near a reading lamp, with his customary Bible in one hand and reading glasses in the other. The William Tell Overture was resounding from the next room, which had a large blanket covering what once was a double-door entryway. I glanced nervously toward the doorway as the announcer said, "Hi-Yo Silver."

Elder Baker said, "I won't hold you long. I will get straight to the point. Did Dolph Rhodes split that storm the other day, or did Deacon Mike?"

By now, I was reconciled with my standard pat answer to inquiries about the storm-splitting incident. "I don't know, sir," was my rehearsed explanation. "I fetched the ax like he told me, but when he raised it up over his head, I think the lightning flashed or something, and I shut my eyes. I don't know what happened."

The Bakers weren't buying it. Sister Baker rose up and in the sweetest voice chimed in. "But, boy, Adolph did have the ax, didn't he? The storm did go around, didn't it?"

My words came out almost a whisper. "Yes, ma'am, he had the ax. I gave it to him."

Elder Baker said, "Now where was Deacon Mike when all this happened?"

Telling the truth freely, I said, "Papa Mike was headed toward the truck. I think he was going to get it so we could go home or outrun the storm or something. He was way away from the cotton choppers."

Chuckling to himself and to Sister Baker, Elder Baker asked rhetorically, "Sure he wasn't going to the truck to hide and leave the madam and the rest of y'all out there in the storm?

"Go on, boy, and watch television. Next time I see Mike, I am going to have a lot of questions about what he was doing when that storm came up. Yes, siree Bob, sir. God done preferred to use a sinner over the top Baptist deacon. You can tell him I said so. Go in there and enjoy yourself."

The room was dimly lit and clustered with perhaps a dozen human bodies all focused on the one seventeen-inch television screen. Although it was twilight outside, my eyes were slow in adjusting to the darkened room. I just stood there in front of the blanket covering the double-wide doorway. My eyes were glued on the Cheerios commercial, awaiting the return of the Lone Ranger.

Something touched my hand. It was thirteen-year-old Cupcake. "I saved your seat over here by me on the love seat."

Temporarily stunned, I hesitated a moment, searching for the right response. All day long, Papa Mike had been saving me from awkward and compromising moments. This time I was on my own. Or so I thought. This time, Carl, sitting on the floor, noticed me and called out, "Hey, Water Boy! Come here. Let me ask you something." Strangely, Carl the Joker didn't stutter or stammer this time, unlike earlier in the week when the storm spilt. Seizing the moment, I eased on down to a sitting position on the floor where four other boys were gathered. Carl and Henry were trying to settle a dispute.

"Water Boy, I've been trying to tell this dodo that the Bible says God made a donkey talk one time. Tell him we had that in Sunday school one Sunday." Not one to cause hurt or harm to anyone, I didn't want to make Joker look good and Henry look bad. I wanted to appease both. I calmly said yes, not wanting to be mixed up in any kind of confrontation. I didn't want Elder Baker to have to poke his head inside the curtain. I also was acutely aware that the commercial break was ending. I wanted to see the masked man and his Indian friend.

"Yes, y'all, the Bible says God made a donkey speak. It also says he can make the rocks cry out. What's up?" I wanted to end it right then and there.

Carl continued while the Lone Ranger and Tonto were sitting around a campfire drinking coffee and talking. I couldn't discern a word they were saying. By now, Dee Dee was in her element, with a second conversation drowning out the TV. Dee Dee was lambasting the Lone Ranger for not ever kissing a woman like the Cisco Kid at the close of his shows. Carl was using the donkey as a way of saying God used Mr. Dolph to split the storm. Cupcake was nudging my backside with her foot, trying to get some attention. Things were not going as I had envisioned.

Springing spryly to my feet, feeling exasperated by the questioning and irritated by the interruptions of my favorite TV show, I said, "Y'all, Mr. Dolph Rhodes split that storm, and all the church folks are upset that God used a sinner man to save us from hurt, harm, and danger." I sat back down. Everybody was as quiet as a church mouse.

Elder Baker, having overheard my disclosure, stuck his head inside the homemade blanket curtain and said to nobody in particular but for all to hear, "God works in mysterious ways. His wonders to perform. Never underestimate God Almighty." With that, he closed the curtain and retreated.

On the screen, the Lone Ranger and Tonto had broken camp and for whatever reason were in hot pursuit of two bad guys. The masked man was astride Hi-Yo Silver while his Indian companion, Tonto, was riding Paint. The bad guys didn't stand a chance. Dee Dee was quiet. Carl was quiet. Henry was quiet. Even Cupcake had stopped playing footsie in the dark. Everybody was looking toward the TV, but I could sense their minds were on storm splitting, saints, and sinners.

CHAPTER 8

GOING TO THE BUSHES: CONFLICT RESOLUTION

"Going to the bushes" was an expected routine and common occurrence. There were no restrooms available for day laborer cotton choppers. The "Port-a-John" was the nearest bolt of Johnson grass, clump of trees, grassy knoll, drudge ditch, or other blinder in sight.

Women wanted to go in pairs—one to watch out for peeping men while the other "used it." Papa Mike tried in vain to discourage pairs. The second woman would only insist that it was her time as well. Some say Mama Rosetta overruled any objection her husband had.

I usually conducted a reconnaissance and selected a suitable spot, preferably one for females. A best-case scenario would be two such places on each end of the quarter-mile-long diametric cotton rows. One was for males, and the other females. Oftentimes it was so.

Cotton leaves were the Charmin of choice, although many adult women carried either tissue paper or pages from a *Sears and Roebuck* catalog in their apron pockets. Otherwise, leaves from any broad-leaved plant would do.

Dee Dee had been on a date, to the picture show with that boy from up on Huff Plantation. They had seen the movie *I Passed for White*. She was sharing her remembrance of the flick from beginning to end, with some omissions. "I couldn't see that part; we were busy doing something else," she would chide.

All the teenagers in her cluster were all ears. It was customary for travelers, moviegoers, book readers, churchgoers, or anyone with a signet experience to share with the group. Esprit de corps and an unwritten culture code dictated that all would listen when one talked. After all, what goes around comes around!

"I cried like a baby when Mahalia Jackson sang that song at the mama's funeral. I believe all the black folks up in the balcony were crying. It's a wonder our tears didn't drown them white folks down under us." Everybody cackled at the thought of harassing white folks in the privileged first-floor-level seats. The colored section was in the balcony upstairs, farther from the big screen.

Carl wasn't called Joker for nothing. He was a master at signifying the art of talking in rhyme while ridiculing an adversary. Signifying was an acceptance form of playing the dozens, which was a rhythmic tirade about somebody's mama.

Cookie was the selected victim of the afternoon. She was dark, short-haired, and rather plump. She was blessed with pleasant feminine facial contours but at the moment was undergoing a case of early teen acne. Carl, for reasons known only to himself, felt compelled to verbally abuse Cookie in a good-natured round of signifying:

> Girl, you so black,
> put you in a croker sack,
> it would look like
> humps on a camel's back.
> Girl, you so fat and greasy
> a gnat could swallow you easy,
> but after dinner he'd beesy
> feeling sick as jungle wind.
> You ugly as homemade sin;
> you break every mirror you look in.

All your family, kit and kin,
wonder what Tarzan movie
you play in.

"Shut your mouth, Joker. You can't say nothing. You are musty, dumb, and your breath smell like dog dookie."

Cookie was hurting, and the more her peers laughed at Carl's tirade against her, the worse she felt. She had to slash back. Cursing was out. Somebody would surely tell her mother, and she would be in deep, deep trouble. Ever since her mother had become a member of the sanctified church, "saints" had to be saints, especially in public.

I eased my left arm around Cookie's shoulders and in a falsetto impression of the Platters sang a bar of "Only You." I knew Carl could be merciless in his signifying. Somehow Cookie seemed too vulnerable. Carl's words were striking too close to home.

"I see the black Lone Ranger done *rid* up to protect you. I guess I'll plant you now and dig you later." Carl and I were real close friends. We got along like two peas in a pod. Now, sensing I wanted him to lighten up, he let Cookie off the hook.

Dimp loved to sing. She had a great sultry soprano voice. Some say it was like Sarah Vaughn's. There was one catch: Dimp was terribly shamed faced and had to hide her face to sing, and then only after intense and persistent urging.

Such was the case this afternoon. After Dee Dee mentioned the crying at Mahalia Jackson's singing in the movie *I Passed for White*, somebody said, "Let's hear Dimp sing it."

Mable pulled off her head scarf. So did Maggie. They dropped their hoes and tucked their two scarves under Dimp's straw hat to make a full veil covering her entire face and neck. She looked like a modified Egyptian mummy or a Moslem woman.

Sweet melodic tones began rising from inside the makeshift veil. She was singing Dinah Washington's "Love Walked in and Drove the Shadows Away." On cue, the other teens started humming the would-be music background. It was moments like this that made me wonder if white folks had this kind of fun. If so, when?

"Mike, tell that boy fetch me a bucket of cool water. Hey, Mike! Hey, Mike! Where is my water?" It was Miss Mills! She was well over eighty, maybe ninety, big, fat, black, and blind. She lived in a green house a mile from the gravel road high on a ridge on the edge of the old Noah place. She sat on the front porch all day. When she wanted something from the store or the well, she bellowed it out to the nearest neighbors. In this case, she could hear the sounds of the day laborers chopping nearly three-quarters of a mile away.

"All right, boy, you heard the blind lady. Take her a full bucket of water and make it snappy. Turn your hat around now. These folks will be hollering for water after a while." Papa Mike, like everybody else, catered to the needs of Miss Mills. She was big-boned, black as tar, and brutally frank. She told everybody off who was two-faced or fake. She could see through make-believe and hypocrisy. It was best to cater to her needs than be ridiculed by a bellowing voice echoing across the flatlands.

I half-trotted all the way to Miss Mills's front porch but kept a watchful eye on the water bucket, which was about four-fifths full. I surely didn't want to incur her wrath and get that much-feared tongue-lashing that everybody feared.

As respectfully as I could, I greeted her with the usual "How you doing, Miss Mills? Want me to pour this water in your fruit jars?"

"Boy, hurrup and put the water in my drinking water pail so I can get me a cool drink. It's hot as a peppered piece of pan trout." She was at her intimidating best.

Miss Mills was notorious for talking loud and booming. She never talked in hushed tones. That is, until now. Throwing the peeking eyes and ears of the cotton choppers off guard, she bellowed in an unpleasant tone, "Boy, this water's warm nuff to bathe a baby! I wanted water off the Chinaman's head."

Then, almost under her breath, she whispered, "Boy, did that sinful Albino split that storm? Tell me the truth now, or I will tan your hide with this raza strop." I looked in her left hand and saw long, black, boney, gaunt fingers clutching a barber's razor strap. My intentions were to speak, but words were slow in coming like molasses in the wintertime.

At first, I was about to rehash the line about lightning flashing and my eyes being shut when Miss Mills changed the razor strap to her right hand and hollered out toward the cotton choppers, "Y'all better come get this boy 'fore I make him blow on this water and cool it!" She raised the razor strap and said again in hushed tones, "Boy, tell me what God loves. I need the truth out of you. I am getting the truth out of you if I have to beat it out."

Words came in a torrent as I let the cat out of the bag. "Yes'sum, he hit the ax in the ground, and the storm went around. It split and went around."

The old blind eyes seemed to twinkle, and a *Mona Lisa*–like smirk flitted across her toothless mouth. She mumbled quietly, "Lord's su'mercy! I knowed it, I knowed it. I knowed it. God's done used a sinner to do his will. Them church folks are upset, ain't they, boy?"

I could only agree. "Yes, ma'am …"

"Water Boy, these folks are waiting on you." It was Papa Mike. This time it was music to my ears, hearing what normally were grating words from the straw boss. I needed to get away from this wise, old, blind black lady. She was too smart for her own good. She made me say what I didn't want to say. I had done more than let the cat out of the bag; I had spilled the beans.

Faking again, Miss Mills hollered out, "Papa Mike, don't send me no mo' bath water. It ain't Sad-day. I wanna cool off, not take a bath. Get on away from here, boy, 'fore I make you fan me."

I took off in my familiar trot, headed back toward the truck to refill the empty bucket from the fifty-five-gallon barrel of water. The ice man ought to hurry up. It was hot.

Mr. Luke was chopping cotton with a decided disadvantage: one arm in a sling. Normally, he was a member of Mama Rosetta's cluster. Not now, not anytime soon. Maybe next year.

The married couple cluster had spilled the beans on how it all happened. His arm was fractured when he threw it up to protect his skull from the path of single-bit ax wielded by his incensed wife. The blade had missed, but the ax handle just below the blade cracked the big bone in his forearm. Mamie Lyons, in belligerent splendor, had tried to behead her husband. The nerve of him, embarrassing her in public.

Word was that Mr. Luke had come to the Juke Joint to ask her—no, tell her—to come home. She was there to see Joe and that new woman he was seeing. Everybody knew that she loved Joe from the top of his shaggy head, down across his round tummy, to the bottom of his pudgy feet. Never mind that he was married with children. Never mind that she was also married and old enough to be his mother. She loved Joe.

Eyewitness accounts had it that he hadn't said a word—just came in, leaned on the bar chewing Juicy Fruit gum and looking. They said she wanted to see who'd been rocking her chair, beating her time. So far, Joe was at a table playing cards with three other men. A couple of strange women were on that side of the Juke Joint, but none seemed interested in Joe.

Of course, I wasn't a fly on the wall for all this, but based on what I have been told over the years, I can pretty much figure out who said what. And, hey, if I'm wrong, I'm wrong.

It's my understanding that Miss Mamie waited. They would show their hand sooner or later. She was in no hurry. Mr. Luke walked in, stopping just inside the door to let his eyes adjust to the dim light. Deacon Luke Lyons was on a mission in the Juke Joint. He had singleness of purpose: to fetch his wife. Heads turned. Activity ceased. Lips dropped. Brows raised. The card game stopped. Dancing came to a halt. Only the jukebox kept on playing. Little Junior Parker was blaring:

> Big fat mama, meat shakes on the bone
> Big fat mama, meat shakes on the bone
> My baby wants me to moan and groan.

"Carrie, get your pocketbook and come on home," Mr. Luke said loud enough to be heard above the jukebox.

It didn't take lipreading to figure out what he was saying. It didn't take expertise in body language to see she was highly perturbed—make that pissed off—by his presence! She became furious and was about to erupt when she noticed total quietness. Junior Parker had finished singing, extolling the virtues of his "big fat mama." The record had ended. Eyewitnesses said all eyes were tuned into the Luke and Mamie show.

She looked around the room, eyes glaring, lingered briefly on Joe, and then bolted for the door. Her husband followed, slowly. She reached it, opened it, swept through, and slammed it in his face. She was going home all right. Just watch! The one, two, threes of the fight leading up to the ax-broken left arm may never be known. What was obvious was that she came close to decapitating her husband for fronting her in public.

Shocked by her own violence, she is said to have cuddled Mr. Luke and screamed for help until neighbors came and got him to town to see the doctor. She never did see Joe's so-called new woman. If he had one, she must have vanished. Miss Mamie was not one to miss. She could have a fit and swing a pretty mean single-bit ax.

I said rather respectfully, "You gonna help Mr. Luke on his row, Miss Mamie!" I could see that the one arm in a sling was hampering Mr. Luke's chopping ability. Miss Mamie was on her usual adjacent row but as usually was chopping fiercely and way ahead of Mama Rosetta and her cluster. She could easily chop some of Mr. Luke's row and maintain a respectable pace.

"Come on here, man. Get your back end up here with your group." She was helping. My nudging had done the trick.

Ben Smith and Ben Parsons were friends and constant companions. They looked like comic book characters Yogi the Bear and Boo-Boo. One was big and tall; the other was short and skinny. During their waking hours, Ben Smith and Ben Parsons were inseparable.

Hulking, lumbering Ben Smith was about fifty years old while his pint-sized road buddy was in his sixties. True to the stereotype, Ben Smith was mostly brawn, while the sly, slick, and sometimes wicked Parsons was the brains of the duo.

Parsons was married to the enterprising Mae Ella Parsons, who was a tightly wired bundle of energy. Both were very articulate and snappy dressers by cotton field standards. They were known to spend two weeks with their two grown children in California during lay-by time.

Ben Smith was single and showed no more than verbal passing interest in women. He lived in the long green house behind the general store with three other families. It was unlikely he had any groceries or other food items in his two-room unit. He ate all his meals with the Parsons. They were a threesome until bedtime.

They chopped cotton the same way every day. Miss Mae Ella Parsons took the first row after Miss Mamie Lyons in the Mama Rosetta cluster. Her husband was next, then Ben Smith. The Parsons were fast talkers and fast choppers. Ben Smith did everything slowly and deliberately, thereby incurring the good-natured wrath of the Parsons, who were constantly nagging him to quicken his pace. They enjoyed one another.

Mama was leader of the mothers with children-in-training cluster. She didn't fit the tenor of the times. She could chop with Mama Rosetta and that cluster, with Ollie Mae and the young grown ones, or with the teenagers if such placement befell her. A mother of ten, she had spent all her time in the mothers with children-in-training cluster.

Her current chore was to give twelve-year-old Billy Boy his final lessons while giving ten-year-old Jean her beginning lessons. Actually, Jean wouldn't be ten until September, but Papa Mike was lenient with near-age children as long as they could and would do the work. One slip, and he was likely to issue a pink slip. He was stern when it came to performance. Everybody respected him for that.

All of Mama's brood were hardworking, churchgoing, well-respected boys and girls. I was not necessarily the apple of her eye. While disclaiming any partiality toward any of her smart children, she counted heavily on the eldest, Carrie, to carry on the family tradition. Carrie was married and living up beyond the Huff Plantation. Son Bob was in Saint Louis with relatives, not because he wanted to but because he had to leave home at age sixteen.

While working at the local cotton gin one night, Bob had been accused of reaching a cotton bale weight ticket across the slumped, asleep body of Jeanette Keyes, white female office clerk. Upon awakening, she said, "That nigger boy was trying to hug me while I was asleep."

The gin manager was compassionate the next day as he related the story to Miss Cora: "I know Bob. He was just doing his job. That crazy woman is going to get somebody killed. I would get rid of her, but her husband would cause trouble."

He paused, looked up at the sky a moment, shook his head, and asked softly, "Cora, is there anywhere Bob could go for a while, like with kinfolks in Clarksdale, Memphis, up north? It's getting rough, and we have to do something before that crazy white woman takes it too far."

Mama was stunned but understood. Her eldest son, age sixteen, had been accused of touching the forbidden fruit—a white woman—and to save his life, he had to leave home. Without further thought, she said, "Thank you, Mr. Paul. Bob is going to Saint Louis!"

Using the telephone in the shop where James worked, she called her deceased first husband's bother in Saint Louis. This prince of a man had offered and begged to adopt all six of his dead brother's children to be raised as his own. Out of a mother's love, Mom had declined the offer on more than one occasion. Yet, Uncle held fast to being a safety net for his nieces and nephews by providing school clothing, a little cash every now and then, and a standing invitation that if any of the children needed help, just ask. His reassuring statement was "That's what kinsfolk are for." In a few days, Bob was in Saint Louis.

Sumner High School in Saint Louis, Missouri, is alma mater of Anna Mae Bullock (aka Tina Turner), Arthur Ashe, Chuck Berry, Grace Bumbry, Dick Gregory, Robert Guillaume, Elston Henry, William Clay, Billy Davis Jr. and James Edward (Bob) Lackey.

Word spread like wildfire that Bob had been falsely accused by that crazy white woman and had to leave home to avoid trouble. Hurried and hushed family meetings were called throughout the black community as parents wanted their children, especially males, to be on their p's and q's around all white women and to stay clear of that crazy white woman.

Bob was graduating from high school in a few weeks. The move to Saint Louis had paid great dividends. He had played on his high school baseball team as a catcher and the football team as a fullback. The Lord works in mysterious ways. His wonders to perform.

Carrie hadn't finished high school, only the tenth grade before marriage and pregnancy, or was it the other way around? Dimp had one more year in school, and I had three. One thing for sure, these children were going to graduate from high school and if any way possible go to college! These cotton fields were not about to kill Mama's dreams. These children would go where she couldn't go right then. One day, the family would be free from that land, and she wanted to live to see it!

Mattie Lee was a practical joker who delighted in Blood Hound chewing tobacco. That wasn't so odd since almost all adult cotton choppers either dipped snuff or chewed one of the prevalent brands of good chewing tobacco. The oddity was Mattie Lee sliced her tobacco razor this and placed it between her bottom lip and snuff.

Rotund and amicable, she could laugh with the best of them. To be in her company was to be giggling, laughing, or howling with joy ere long. She was a gas.

One shortcoming: she had her eyes on a married tractor driver. Her own significant other—it was never determined whether she had been married or shacking—was still up north around Gary, Indiana. Mattie Lee had gone up there to visit but met this "wonderful man" and had stayed six years. Now, she was back chopping cotton and not letting on as to how long she was going to stay with her parents or what.

Be that as it may, she was having a ball being among the young married cotton choppers. Word was, come Saturday night, she turned things up a notch with the tractor driver. Gossip was like vinegar on greens; life just tasted better when sprinkled with gossip!

Gene and Gertie Matthews were chopping in the married with children-in-training cluster with Miss Cora and her children. This had caused quite a stir on three accounts. First, Gene and Gertie were nearly fifty years of age. Second, their little girl was "little" but passing for age ten. And third, the child was almost white!

Gertie was not the biological mother. The little girl had been entrusted to the Matthews to raise and cherish, so they said, by the girl's mother. What they never would say was whether the girl's mother was white and the father black or whether the girl's mother was black and the father white.

One thing is for sure, I thought to myself. There was a dead cat on the line somewhere; the girl was 90 percent white and 10 percent black.

Gene and Gertie began speaking in hushed tones when Mr. Jake came to get Ollie Mae. Mama evidently couldn't hear what they were saying. She looked around, caught my attention, and gave me an all too familiar mother-to-son gesture. "Check this out."

I eased over to where the mothers were chopping and asked coyly, "Do you three want any water?" They did, but no other talk beyond small talk in my presence.

Dee Dee was stout, short of stature, short-haired, and rather plain until she straightened her hair and applied the reddest lipstick she could find. The Maggie red lips, black face, and off-center gold tooth gave her smiling countenance a peculiar mystique. She carried herself with arrogance and confidence. That is, unless she was caught off guard and upstaged. It happened.

Dimp was laughing and cajoling with the rest as Dee Dee related the highlights of her movie date with the boy from up on the Huff Plantation. In an ill-advised outburst, Dimp asked Dee Dee, "He didn't puke up when he kissed you, did he?"

Shock waves seemed to go through Dee Dee. Flashes of hurt followed by waves of rage must have zinged through her nervous system. She was virtually traumatized. She was hurt. She was embarrassed. *How did Dimp know?* she must have wondered. *Did Bob tell that awful secret to his sister? Did he tell anybody else?*

I knew about her secret. "It" had happened one night during the Christmas holidays while Bob was visiting from Saint Louis.

They had been walking the short distance from the general store to Dee Dee's home, taking their time, arm in arm. She felt warm and fuzzy, basking in the attention Bob was giving her. After all, he played football for Sumner High School in Saint Louis. Nobody, absolutely nobody else in all of Quitman County played football. She felt special. She wanted icing on her cake.

Assertive and forward in her demeanor, she went ahead and told Bob, "Kiss my red lips." In all the time that has gone by, a certain realm of speculation just went bust. People talk. I listen. I now know for a fact that her memory had been hibernating in a self-protective amnesia. For the life of her, she couldn't remember, didn't want to remember what happened after she asked Bob to kiss her. Hearsay had it that Bob looked down at her in a manner suggesting he was willing to comply with her demand issued in a requesting tone. He gathered her in his arms; this she vaguely remembered.

Then, suddenly his body lurched, and he began regurgitating vile, sour-smelling vomit.

He was puking!

The thought of kissing her Maggie red, juicy lips backed by an off-centered gold tooth had evoked vomit?

Stunned. Petrified. She became concerned for his health and well-being, then insulted, hurt, and embarrassed as realization sank in. The thought of kissing her had made him puke!

Now, his sister had the audacity to ask her whether the boy from up on Hough had puked during the kissing episode in the movie balcony.

Dee Dee tried to mask her feelings by continuing to chop cotton. She attacked a cluster of Johnson grass with such rage that the hoe skipped and cut through her flip-flops, slicing the big toe on her right foot. She screamed in anguish. "Look what you made me do! You made me cut my foot."

In a swift motion, she raised her hoe skyward, stepped wildly across the three rows between herself and Dimp, and brought the hoe down sharply. She fully intended to kill the sister of the boy who puked and told. It was bad enough to kiss and tell but to puke and tell ...

Dimp was not ready for the attack. In a feeble and futile attempt at self-protection, she put up her left arm, but the hoe landed just above her left eye. All of us nearby heard the crush of metal on bone. She fell to the ground in a twisted heap of fear. We all grimaced as blood spewed from seared skin, like air hissing from a punctured balloon. We thought death was nigh at hand.

Mind you, at that age, I was a great lover of comic book and biblical heroes, especially those with dual identities; meek and mild mannered while in disguise but brave, strong, and daring when cloaked in hero's attire! I especially identified with those who swooped in to rescue damsels in distress. This distressed damsel was no ordinary endangered lass; this was my sister! Like a madman, I swung into action!

I had seen Dee Dee, with the raised hoe, step across three cotton rows and swing the hoe down on my sister. Too far away to stop the onslaught, I had screeched, "Dee Dee! Dee Dee! What are you doing!" as I dropped the water bucked and streaked superhero fashion across the twenty or so cotton rows to Dee Dee and Dimp.

Too late. The initial blow had been struck. Dee Dee raised the hoe for a second time. No way was I going to let her hit my sister a second time. I gathered all the strength I could and with a surge that would make Batman proud slithered through the air and caught Dee Dee about the knees, knocking her off balance, and we both fell across cotton stalks to the ground. The hoe went sailing as our bodies sprawled.

Onlookers were screaming and hollering in shock, fear, disbelief, and heightened concern.

Mama rushed to the side of her daughter, crying, "Be-Bee done kilt my baby. Dee Dee done kilt my baby."

The other teenagers were gathering around, fidgeting, falling over one another, trying to help stop the bleeding and trying to understand what had happened. They didn't know about Bob and the puking. Only Dimp and Dee Dee knew.

Meanwhile, Rayford Charles had come over to help Carl and Mable pull me off Dee Dee, who was being flailed at unmercifully. My mild-mannered meekness as Water Boy had been transformed into a fist-flailing, blows-raining, vengeful maniac. I was trying to beat the hell out of Dee Dee, despite her bleeding toe, Maggie red lips, and off-centered gold teeth. They got me off Dee Dee while she was still alive.

The hoe had made a glancing blow that sliced through the skin, leaving a two-inch horizontal gash on Dimp's head. Snuff was packed on the gash to retard the bleeding and covered with the underside of several cotton leaves so as not to use poisonous top sides. Makeshift bandages were made, strips taken from Miss Parson's apron.

Papa Mike told Miss Cora to take Dimp home.

Everybody was relieved that she wasn't more seriously hurt. It could easily have been a fatal wounding.

Dee Dee was seething. She had scared herself. She couldn't explain to anybody's satisfaction why she had attacked Dimp. "She was making fun of me!" But nobody could substantiate that. The sidebar question of "did he puke" was almost unnoticed by the other teenagers since it had no meaning to them.

Papa Mike told Dee Dee to pick up her hoe and go home. He was suspending her for the time being.

Now sulking and not showing any outward remorse, Dee Dee put the hoe on her shoulder and started walking home. She was trying.

CHAPTER 9

EVERYBODY HAS A STORY

Old Man Will Tanner and Mr. Harry Wilson joined me on the last three rows at the beginning of each cotton-chopping start-up. I understood why I had the very last row. It would always be me who would stop chopping and begin delivering water after the first two hours in the morning and the first hour in the afternoon. The other two were different stories. Mr. Tanner suffered from mobility issues associated with one leg being shorter than the other. Mr. Walker chopped with his right hand in the front pocket of his trousers.

Both men shared their respective stories with me, as did most choppers at one time or another. Maybe I was a sounding board or story bank. Sometimes the stories were too personal, too grown-up, or too close to home.

Old Man Tanner told in several different episodes how he was born short-legged and was a misfit among his childhood peers. He had what is today known as leg length discrepancy, which is when one's two legs are of unequal lengths. Experts estimate that 85 percent of the world's population has one leg that's longer than the other, albeit miniscule. A slight difference in limb length is usually indistinguishable and unnoticed. However, when the difference is multiple inches between legs, a lift has to be inserted into that shoe's outsole to even out the shorter leg's length. Mr. Tanner had at least an added four inches under the shoe on his left foot.

He didn't have the corrective shoe until he was eighteen years old and drafted by the military. He failed the physical and was sent home, but something good came about anyway. Although he was classified IV-F, the intake official recommended he see a foot doctor and get measured for a lifted sole shoe.

He told me how, when growing up, his siblings would run ahead and leave him in the dark when walking home at night from visiting neighbors, from church, or just strolling. He became leery of accompanying family members on nighttime excursions. He stayed home more often than not. Walking from church or school during daylight had hazards as well. Almost every household had a passel of dogs who felt it their appointed duty to not only protect the yard and house but also the road near the house. I knew this all too well. Seemingly, watchdogs had their version of a no-fly zone or a twelve-mile limit."

The story got a little raunchy when Old Man Tanner lapsed into how he couldn't catch up with the fast girls growing up, but he couldn't outrun them either. Chuckling with a telltale wink, he often shared how, as a young man, "fast girls" caught up with him and he was glad to be "crippled."

Fittingly, I resisted the urge to respectfully inquire about later years, grown-up years. Old Man Tanner was a widower with several grown children and a wide age range of young grandchildren. Apparently, his lifted shoe had enhanced his catch-up abilities, or somebody caught up with him on more than one occasion. I just had to smile when thinking off-limits thoughts about grown-ups' secret business.

Mr. Harry Wilson was relatively new to the local area, having relocated from down near Inverness. He was extremely private and stayed to himself on and off the field. He also lived alone in one of the smaller, one-room green houses behind the general store. He had two attention-attracting oddities. First, he chopped cotton with one hand, his left hand, while the right hand was stuffed in his right front pocket and the hoe handle lodged in the curve of his right arm. The second oddity was embarrassing: the crotch area of his trousers was always wet, and when close, had the telltale and unmistakable pungent smell of urine. Mr. Harry, as he was called, had serious plumbing problems.

Everybody wondered but nobody knew what was going on with Mr. Harry. That is, nobody knew except Old Man Tanner and me. I wished many a day that I did not know. Knowing Mr. Harry's story gave me shudders. Plus, people, suspecting I knew, invariably asked what was wrong with Mr. Harry.

The story had been told not in the cotton fields but on the porch of Mr. Harry's little green house behind the general store during one of my Saturday-afternoon *Grit* newspaper delivery stops. Mr. Harry was not a regular customer. Nevertheless, he hailed me and invited me to bring a paper and then invited me to have a seat on the porch.

Sensing something confidential was about to transpire, I felt ill at ease from the beginning. I handed Mr. Harry the newspaper, took the dime, and sat in the cane-bottom straight-back chair. I turned the chair from its angle to face the gravel road so as to avoid looking in the direction of my host. Mr. Harry had the chairs pre-positioned where they were almost facing each other. He now sat facing me in the other cane-bottom straight-back chair. His right hand was in his right front pants pocket, and the smell of urine punctuated the air. I fought the urge to see whether his trousers had that telltale wet spot. I had purposely not allowed my eyes to drift near the crotch area of the faded blue coveralls. My mind wandered momentarily as I debated whether the garment was coveralls or overalls. The vernacular was perplexing. I had done it again: used a big word from my stepfather's comprehensive encyclopedia.

Mr. Harry was asking me a question. "Boy, I heah tell you is a Christian. Am I right or wrong?

"Yes, sir," I said while still facing the gravel road. Reverend Longmire had always said Christians should speak up and identify themselves. In Matthew 10:32, Jesus says, "Whosoever therefore shall confess me before men, him will I confess also before my Father which is in heaven."

"Well, boy, let me tell you why my britches is pissy and I have to hold my family package in my hand all times. It's gonna sound real grown like, but I want you to know. Them there laughing and snickering hoe hands from Mama Rosetta's bunch to everybody except your mama just about to get under my skin. I want you to know my business so you can tell them to let me alone and mind their own business. Tell them if you have to, but if you don't feel like it, let it go. Old Man Tanner already knows. He is my only friend. Papa Mike and Dolph don't make no never mind.

"It all started down there near Inverness in a place called Isola when I was driving tractors five and six days a week and singing with B.B. King on Saturday nights at lay-by time. I am sure you heard of B.B., but there were others of us too. There was Little Milton Campbell and Albert King who both played guitar. Course, Albert was left-handed and played his guitar upside down. There was this juice harp player, Little Arthur Duncan, who was with us. We had it pretty good. The ladies fell all over they-selves trying to get to us. I must confess—we didn't try too hard to fight them off."

I was fidgeting with the *Grit* newspaper bag and nervously pulled one copy out and put it back into the bag.

"Well, word got out that God had blessed me with a family package a bit larger than most other men. I don't know about that, but I enjoyed the notoriety. Women smiled and flirted with me all the time, wherever we played. Some even got the nerve to come out to the cotton fields where I be plowing. Yes, sir, word got around that I was like Sampson or Goliath, I don't remember which."

Mr. Harry's self-disclosure made me think about my own peers and how word was out that Carl the Joker was more physically endowed than the rest of us. I was wondering what difference such things would make when Mr. Harry answered question.

"My boss man had lost his first wife to consumption, TB, or something like that. He remarried this gold-digging, young, pretty thing from up in Memphis. Well, one day he was waiting when I parked my tractor and fueled it up with butane for the next day. He come striding up to me and says, 'Harry, if you can keep your trap shut and not tell anybody, I can let you make two days' wages for one hour's work.'

"I ain't exactly money hungry, but working for four bits an hour for twelve hours and making six dollars a day and then being offered twelve dollars for an hour of honest labor sounds pretty good. Right, boy?"

Eager to know what was coming next, I said respectfully, "Yes, sir. It surely does." I felt bad for having said does rather than do. I had read the Bible from cover to cover in two years, starting from my eleventh birthday and ending on my thirteenth birthday. I then turned right around and read it again from Genesis to Revelation before my fourteenth birthday. I was quite adept with subject and verb agreement in the English language. Yet, I didn't ever want to sound and act greater than any of my peers, church members, or fellow cotton choppers. Certainly, I didn't want to upstage any grown-ups.

Warming up and thinking I was on safe footing, I gathered courage, turned in the general direction of Mr. Harry, and ventured a question. "What did you have to do for an hour?" Immediately as the words rolled off my lips, I knew somehow I had overstepped the bounds between comfort and discomfort. The words wouldn't come back.

"Well, boy," Mr. Harry said in lowered to hush tones, "that sickly old white man wanted me to be in a family way with his young wife. Boss man said he had heard I was blessed like some old stallion, and he wanted me to do what he couldn't do."

My inner being lapsed automatically in a defense mode, and I instinctively rose and looked down the front steps leading to the gravel road. Mr. Harry reached out with his left hand and in a gentle manner said firmly, "Sit down and listen, boy. I need you to hear this."

Obediently, I sat back down in the cane-bottom straight-back chair. My gaze was riveted to the pine-knotted floor. I wished I was home or, better yet, grown!

Mr. Harry continued with his story. "I bristled at that old man and was about to ask him whether he was drunk or crazy when he pulled out that pistol. I don't know whether it was a .38, .45, or what. All I know is he pulled a gun on me and said I had a choice: get my head blown off or do as he asked me.

"We went over to his house, and he made me sit down in an old horse trough and take a cold-water bath with my clothes on. I was wet as hell. I was nervous as hell. He made me pull off my clothing and threw me an old horse blanket to cover myself. Then he made me walk into his house.

"I won't burden your young brain with the details, but evidently they had discussed it, and she was waiting for me. It was the worst feeling I ever had in my life. But somehow, it happened. When it was over, I stumbled out of their bedroom, and there stood boss man with a sawed-off shotgun this time. I just knew I was dead. I threw up both hands and was about to plead for my life when he swung the butt of the shotgun right into my groin area, and the pain knocked me unconscious.

"When I woke up, maybe after half an hour—I don't rightfully know—I was on the ground outside the house near that horse trough, with wet clothing piled on top of me. I looked up and slowly remembered where I was and what I had done and what had been done to me. I jumped up and ran with my clothes in my hand."

The story was intriguing despite being too risqué for my self-awareness. I wanted to hear the rest but hoped for a happy ending.

"Boy, I found my way up here. I left my own good woman and three chilluns down there in Isola. I am not a man anymore. How can I face my family? I am more like a gelding or a hog that has been castrated."

Biblical scripture came to mind. I remembered reading in Matthew 19:12, where Jesus says, "There are eunuchs who were born that way, and there are eunuchs who have been made eunuchs by others—and there are those who choose to live like eunuchs for the sake of the kingdom of heaven. The one who can accept this should accept it."

For the first time, I looked Mr. Harry in the face. Momentarily, we were equally two colored males of the species, understanding and yet not understanding the southern way of life. I rose and descended the steps leading to the gravel road. Mr. Harry said quietly, "That's my story."

CHAPTER 10

Generations of Australians, Canadians, and Americans grew up waiting for the Raleigh man to arrive at their front door with his sample case of goodies to add spice to their life and heal their ailments.

The Raleigh man brought to family front doors the best materials money could buy from around the world: spices from Sumatra, Java, China, India, Africa, the West Indies; black pepper from the island of Ponapai; lemon and orange oils from California and Sicily; vanilla from Madagascar and Java; high-grade coffee beans from the Andes.

In April 1889, against his father's wishes, eighteen-year-old Will Raleigh set out to make his fortune selling medicines door-to-door with a mortgaged buggy, an old blind horse named Bill, and a rig on time payment.

Within three years, he had paid for a good horse, a new wagon, and all his freight and living expenses. He had bought a new home and furnished it and had several good rigs and everything needed with which to conduct his business.

A Raleigh man made frequent and regular visits to the Sabino Plantation, also known as Garmon Farms. He was white. He was friendly. He liked black women.

Maggie had been a virtual child bride, not really unusual for the general populace but quite so in her case. Born to parents with a steady income and with bloodlines touching black bourgeois, Maggie had a bright future. That is, until she fell in love, got married, and had three children by her seventeenth birthday.

She met James in the sixth grade. He had been three years her senior but held back in lower grades for lack of school attendance. He worked part-time on weekends and sometimes after school. By contemporary standards, he had money, and he lavished it on her. She had more than her share of candies, beads, lockets, rings, and scarves and a good lunch every day.

James wanted more. He wanted Maggie whole soul and body. It was the body part that worried her the most. She had just turned thirteen, and her body was showing the telltale signs of adolescence. Mother Nature had started to make a monthly house call, and the bras she had worn for the last two years were beginning to fulfill their purpose.

While delivering *Grit* newspapers on Saturdays, I often overheard Miss Jenna loud talking and giving advice. "Don't let them boys sweet-talk you. Go to school get a good education. Go up north and make something out of yourself." Older sister Lula had said you could "do it" and not get pregnant if you douched with vinegar soon after being with a boy. Plus, James kept saying he would "pull it" and not get her pregnant. I can imagine Maggie was torn between should she or should she not?

That question was answered all by itself without a moment of hesitancy when one rainy night they were parked under that large pecan tree in James's mother's yard.

Maggie herself just blurted out to me one day, "It just happened. No planning. No begging. No nothing. It just happened." Mind you, this sort of talk made me most uncomfortable. Anything remotely related to sex and said in the open, whether one-on-one or in a group, gave me discomfort. It just seemed like sex was designed to be the ultimate privacy act. After all, parents, preachers, teachers, and old folks never mentioned it.

Nine months later. While still thirteen, she had Winston. Then along came Christopher, and then Irene, and finally Tony. Three children by the age of seventeen, four before she was twenty. Dreams were dashed. Her mother was devastated—not openly but nonetheless heartbroken.

She and James made a nice living for themselves and their children by local standards. He worked twelve to eighteen hours a day, six days a week. They went to church on Sundays.

Social life was confined to being in bed from midnight to dawn—period.

Maggie was restless. She longed to be a free and easy teenager. Heck, she longed to chop cotton with people her own age. Instead, James only allowed her to chop half days on Tuesdays and Thursdays. He wanted her to stay close and take care of the children. He would make the money.

What about social interaction? What about being lonely? What about hugging and loving before midnight? What about dancing? Joy riding? She was living like an old woman before age twenty.

The Raleigh man pulled up in his panel truck with bottles and boxes of Raleigh products. These ranged from candy, to rat poison, to perfumes.

He was a squat little white man with a short-sleeved white shirt, narrow brim hat, and brown loafers. He had a quick smile, an easy manner, and shifty eyes. His distinguishing features were his being double-jointed with huge hands, especially his oversized fingers.

Maggie knew about the Raleigh man. Every black woman had heard how he drove around selling products and buying favors, sexual favors, from isolated black woman.

From her porch, Maggie could see and hear the choppers about a quarter of a mile away. They were close enough to hear a call for help yet far enough away not to know what was going on if she had something to hide.

She smiled at the Raleigh man. "Now, what do you have on special this week? Something pretty?"

The Raleigh man glanced about, surveying the isolation, and spoke in the loud and rehearsed voice of a veteran salesman. "I have some of that tonic water for ladies and that Hadacol for colds. That's good stuff, four bits a bottle. Could I get you some?"

I was refitting the bucket from the spigot at the bottom of the fifty-five-gallon water barrel when I saw the dust-covered truck of the Raleigh man stop at James and Maggie's house. I admired cousin James for his braggadocio, genius as an auto mechanic, gustiness as a gospel singer, and most of all, for having the courage to get married early.

The exploits of the Raleigh man were legendary. He preyed on poor black women who snickered and giggled but never complained to parents, husbands, or authorities about being harassed.

The spigot was emitting water at a snail's pace as usual, so I climbed up onto the truck. From this vantage point, I saw the Raleigh man enter the house with Maggie.

"Doggone it," I thought aloud. "White men got all the white woman and still want colored girls." Nah, not Maggie. Surely the Raleigh man was only going to get a look at some floor stain or other area needing special cleaning. Surely …

I couldn't console myself with those thoughts as time ticked away. I jumped down from the bed of the truck, turned the faucet off, took a quick look at Papa Mike standing on his hoe handle across the way, and took off for the bushes. Everybody had to go to the bushes to relieve themselves sooner or later in the course of a half day of work. Water Boys were no different.

I was going to the bushes to relieve myself. I passed one, two, three clumps of tall Johnson grass. I wanted to get a good angle on cousin James and Maggie's house. I wanted to see what the Raleigh man was up to today.

What I heard stopped me dead in my tracks. I heard shrieks coming from the open window. A woman's voice was emitting shrill sounds.

Were they cries for help?

My first thoughts were to rescue Maggie from the fell clutches of the Raleigh man. Looking about, seeing a broken piece of concrete from an old house site, I grabbed it and walked briskly the final fifty yards or so to the house.

I hurled the concrete chunk high above the house where it hit near the chimney with a *thunk*. Turning on my heels, I bolted in the direction of the Chevrolet. Tears streamed down. *What in the world is going on? Are these the last days? Is the world coming to an end?*

Panting, chest burning from the forcing of oxygen into overwrought lungs, I arrived at the truck and turned the faucet to resume the slow filling of the bucket.

"Lord, grant I the serenity." Then I stopped, wiping my tears.

In the distance, the Raleigh man was speeding for the main road that led to the general store. Normally, he stopped near the choppers and whiled away the time, bilking gullible choppers-turned-shoppers for their hard-earned cash with his "specials." Not so today, much to the surprise of Miss Parsons, his favorite customer. "Glory be to God, I guess he has some place to be." She sniffed, disappointedly.

I was busy looking over at the long green house to get a glimpse of Maggie. She was nowhere in sight, although I could imagine her peeping through the flowing curtains just inside the open window in the middle room.

I found myself smiling with a degree of satisfaction as the dust cloud behind the Raleigh man's panel truck turned to a fading wisp.

Whatever the Raleigh man had in mind changed all of a sudden when that concrete hit the top of the house. *Probably scared the stuffing out of both of them*, I thought. I decided then and there not to tell James or anybody. It would probably never happen again.

Those full and rich days of 1957 still seem as if they just passed only yesterday, yet it has been decades. My life has ebbed and flowed, and now I recollect the funniest of things, like the story behind Hadacol. Hadacol was a patent medicine marketed as a vitamin supplement. Its principal attraction, however, was that it contained 12 percent alcohol (listed on the tonic bottle's label as a "preservative"), which made it quite popular in the dry counties of the southern United States. It was the product of four-term Louisiana State Senator Dudley J. LeBlanc, a Democrat from Abbeville in Vermilion Parish in southwestern Louisiana. He was not a medical doctor, nor a registered pharmacist, but had a strong talent for self-promotion.

LeBlanc created the name Hadacol from his former business, the Happy Day Company, maker of Happy Day Headache Powders (which had been seized by the Food and Drug Administration) and Dixie Dew Cough Syrup. Happy became HA, Days became DA, Company became CO, and his own last name, LeBlanc, provided the L. Hence the created name Hadacol. However, when LeBlanc was asked about the name, he would often joke, "Well, I hadda call it something!" ("Medicine: The Mixture as Before," *Time*, January 22, 1951).

Having spendable cash money for Hadacol, alcohol, or any other elixir was problematic. Cash beyond funds for necessities was rare. The number one excess was 12 bits.

Every Saturday morning was when private landowners, townspeople, children still in school, and folks with other jobs came to chop five hours and make themselves $1.50 by eleven in the morning. These newcomers at various times were called Dollar and Four Bitters, Twelve Bitters, or Dollar and Four Bits Choppers. Here is why.

In the United States, the bit is equal to one-eighth of a dollar, or 12.5 cents. Thus, a quarter is two bits, a half dollar is four bits. One dollar and a half is equal to 12 bits. In the US, the "bit" as a designation for money dates from the colonial period, when the most common unit of currency used was the Spanish dollar, also known as "piece of eight," which was worth eight Spanish silver reales. One-eighth of a dollar or one silver real was one "bit."

With the adoption of the decimal US currency in 1794, there was no longer a US coin worth one-eighth of a dollar, but "two bits" remained in the language with the meaning of one-quarter dollar, "four bits" half dollar, and so on. Because there was no one-bit coin, a dime (ten cents) was sometimes called a short bit and fifteen cents a long bit.

The normal thirty to thirty-two field hands easily expanded to fifty or even seventy-five if a busload from Clarksdale came. Everybody who was anybody wanted to be in the field on Saturday to intermingle with the visitors. This Saturday was extra special. The visitors were full of questions, and the regulars all had answers. As the saying goes, those who knew weren't talking, and those who were talking didn't know. Papa Mike, Mr. Dolph, and I were tightlipped. Everybody else was talking up a storm.

I was always intrigued by the Saturday influx of choppers. First of all, Papa Mike promoted me to an administrative position at the start of the day. No longer did I have to chop until the first call for water around seven thirty or eight. I was assisting Papa Mike, making sure the newcomers clustered themselves with the appropriate groups. This was especially applicable to mothers with apprentice children. But it was also important that teenagers were with teenagers, married and unmarried young adults were together, fast choppers were with Mama Rosetta, and extremely slow or needing-isolation choppers were with Old Man Tanner and Mr. Harry.

Dolph Rhodes filed hoes differently on Saturdays. He hit a hoe a lick and a promise as he made his rounds. Instead of filing the blades to a thin cutting edge, he rubbed across it a couple of times with the emery file and was through. Choppers joked that Mr. Dolph was doing a "quickie" or "hit and run just for fun."

Nobody complained. The quick filing was hardly needed in the first place. The cotton fields selected for Saturday chopping were usually the fields less in need of chopping. The foreman would select such fields and not entrust the cotton fields requiring painstakingly laborious chopping to these visitors. The townspeople were notorious for being inept at careful chopping, and word was many of them would purposefully chop down the cotton and leave the grass.

Still, it was an exciting time. Jealous girls and women wanted to watch their significant others. Philandering young men, excitable boys, and dirty old men were window-shopping as the townswomen descended the steps of the old school bus. These country males fantasized making rendezvous with city females later on Saturday evening on Issaquena Avenue in Clarksdale. Sometimes it happened, but most times it didn't. The age-old question arose time and again: "Why does the dog chase the cat?" It must be genetic.

Every group was talking back and forth about the storm and storm splitting. Early Wright had been talking about it on WROX radio in Clarksdale. The "Loud Mouth of the South," as he dubbed himself, had said, "The folks out on the Sabino Plantation witnessed a miracle as a storm was split by a preacher with an ax." Newcomers were wanting to know who was the preacher. Well, every regular chopper was saying it was not a preacher but the hoe filler who sold moonshine whiskey. This naturally created questions for which there were no answers.

Personally, I had other thoughts and was fantasizing about a rendezvous with a certain bus-riding damsel cotton chopper on Issaquena Avenue later that evening. She was about my age and had on a long white shirt, clean blue jeans, and a large straw hat. She wasn't particularly pretty but was an upgrade over Dee Dee, Cookie, and yes, Cupcake. She was bilaterally symmetric. There, I did it again—had thoughts in textbook terms. I was walking toward her and debating with myself as to whether bilateral symmetry meant the dorsal and ventral sides were identical. If so, that was a misnomer. (Drats! I was still doing it.) This girl's backside and her front side were certainly not identical. Her back was flat and straight until below the waist. There, it ... Could I be thinking dirty? The front was barely discernible under the bulky shirt, but she was a girl all right, coming into womanhood.

Feeling older than my years from the several encounters with grown-ups over the week, I surprised myself by not being shy when I said without rehearsing, "You had better get your water first before the snuff dippers start calling me."

She looked up, surprised but not startled. "You got that right. That's so thoughtful of you." She was speaking in a friendly but loud voice so her two peers could hear. She then turned to them and advised, "Y'all had better get your water now before all those toothless mouths salivate all over the dipper."

One of them retorted, "You are sure right, Bernice ..."

That's all I needed to hear was her name. Taking into consideration that it was only just after seven o'clock, I figured I would be back to bring her water three or maybe even four more times before eleven. I could quietly and slowly get around to "Are you going to be on

88

Issaquena Avenue tonight?" I had a plan! I was working on my favorite word ... rendezvous!

Strangely, neither Bernice nor her two friends mentioned the storm and its splitting. Maybe the topic was not as hot as I once believed. Or maybe they were carried away with me and forgot everything else. I strutted toward Mama Rosetta and her bunch without being called. I felt good about having a non-cotton-chopping responsibility. I wondered whether trusties among prisoners felt superior to other prisoners even though they were all in the same boat. Hadn't slaves, especially house slaves, felt superior to field slaves? I felt a need to read slaves' narratives. I started thinking, *Not a one of us is free until all of us is free. So until all cotton choppers are relived of this burden, my soul will not rest.*

We had to dig Ms. Bessie's grave on Saturday afternoon. Grave digging was an eerie yet necessary undertaking. Able-bodied men and strapping teenage boys were asked to form grave-digging teams. Close relatives were excused.

The grave site team consisted of four or five males who piled into a car or on the back of a truck and traveled the three miles to Paw-Paw Cemetery located at Pleasant Grove M.B. Church on Mississippi Highway 6.

There, a site was identified, cleared off, and outlined, and a three-by-six-foot hole was dug into the bowels of the Delta mud. Two people dug in tandem until a depth of three feet or so when only one could work at a time. Therefore, one person used a spade to dig and toss clods of dirt up and out of the pit.

There was something most discomforting about being in the pit once three feet had been reached. It seemed too constraining, too much like being in a grave. I couldn't stand it. Somehow they rigged the rotation that put me in the last foot or so. The other men knew that being that deep bothered me and made jokes about an "early grave," "rising again," and "letting the dead bury the dead." I was glad when it was determined that the grave was finished. For the longest of moments, I lingered in the pit before two men finally reached down, caught my shovel handle, and hoisted me aloft.

There would be no trip to Clarksdale this Saturday night. The events of the week and the grave digging had tuckered me out. I just didn't feel like taking a bath in the number 3 tub, putting on ironed blue jeans, hitching a ride, and most of all answering questions about storm splitting. I could imagine that's all everybody wanted to talk about.

My goodness, I told Bernice, that new girl cotton chopper from Clarksdale, I would be walking down Issaquena Avenue tonight! Torn between adventure and fatigue, I never concluded what I would do. Nature decided for me as I feel fast asleep, sprawled across the bed in the friendly confines of the boys' empty room. Everybody but me was out and about. It was Saturday night live, and I was slumbering.

CHAPTER 11

LIFE-CHANGING SERMON

I was sitting in my customary seat on the front row of the right-hand seats facing forward, next to the three deacons' rows that faced across the church. I was wondering how the seating custom developed. The choir in the choir stand made sense. The pulpit and the rostrum made sense. Even the mothers in the mothers' board seats and deacons in the deacons' seats made sense. What was puzzling was the seating in the three rows of pews facing the pulpit.

Ushers' Room ←Exit	Piano ←	↓Choir↓		Pastors' Study Exit→
Usher	Assistant pastor	**Pulpit** Pastor↓	Visiting minister	Usher
First Lady→		**Rostrum**		←Head deacon
Mothers→		Collections table or		←Deacons
Mothers→		Devotional table or		←Deacons
Mothers→		(Funeral casket)		←Deacons

Left Row↑	aisle	Center Row↑	aisle	Right Row↑
Mostly older women		Married couples with children and young women		Older men Young men
Usher	Usher	**Entrance**	Usher	Usher

Older women sat in the left-hand row of pews. Married women with children and sometimes their husbands sat in the middle rows, as did all children. Older men and boys old enough to be by themselves sat on the right-hand side.

For funerals, relatives occupied the middle row, taking as many pews as needed. The rest of the seating arrangements were abbreviated, with all women folk moving to the left and all men folk to the right. Weddings were different. Mothers and deacons' seats were yielded to the wedding party. Almost all seating arrangements became impromptu. But on pastoral Sundays, the customary seating arrangements were adhered to rigidly.

Rev. H. W. Longmire was preaching his sermon on pastoral day, which for Friendship Church was the second Sunday in each month. He pastored Centennial Baptist Church in Clarksdale on the first and third Sundays. This Sunday, his text was "God Is a Just God."

First Corinthians 10:13 says, "No temptation has seized you except what is common to man. And God is faithful; he will not let you be tempted beyond what you can bear. But when you are tempted, he will also provide a way out so that you can stand up under it."

The pastor made it plain and simple: "God gives us problems and answers at the same time. When faced with problems, we often fail to see the answers because we place artificial barriers between ourselves and the solutions that God gives us." He went on to say that these barriers may be self-pity, pride, fear, laziness, or just plain old doubt.

As usual, Reverend Longmire punctuated his sermon with the Baptist preacher voice inflections that had the deacons saying in unison, "Yeah!" "Go 'head now!" "Preach!" and "Amen!" and mesmerized the mothers of the church who tried their level best to impress the first lady with their responses. Some mothers were chorusing the deacons, while others, when getting in a word edgewise, would chime in with their own created retorts. For instance, everyone was waiting for Sister Dawkins to say, "I know that's right!" Sister Ruth would sooner or later say, "Shut your mouth!"

And finally, Sister Sissy Simpson was going to rise at the right moment and fling her purse at the pastor. Some questioned whether or not this was staged or authentic, but with the contents of the purse being strewn hither and thither, it was generally agreed that this was no faking. Just why she did such a thing was never satisfactorily understood. Once the purse was thrown, Sister Simpson would make a beeline toward the pulpit, fully intending to accost the pastor. Deacons and ushers were on the lookout, and to the disappointment of almost everyone, they would stop her just in time. Everybody wondered what she would do to or with the pastor if she ever got to him.

I was oblivious to these activities as Reverend Longmire drained the sermon for all he could get out of it. The notion that God was a just God and never put on each of his children more than they could bear was comforting. The notion that God gave his children problems and answers always at the same time was mind-boggling. Whatever problem Christians had always had a ready-made solution? Wow! Then what was the catch? Why did people struggle and hassle so? Why didn't problems get solved?

Reverend Longmire was explaining.

"Old pride gets in our way. It builds a blinder right there between our problem and God's answer. Old pride won't let us see. Pride tells us we will look like a fool. Old pride whispers in our ear and tells us folks gonna laugh at us. Old pride tells us that such actions are below our dignity.

"Fear raises its ugly head and tells us if we step out on his Word, we are foolish. We are gonna fail. Fear tells us we don't have the money. We don't have the talents. We don't have the wherewithal to make things happen. Fear tells us it's better to be safe than sorry. Fear tells us we are gonna suffer terrible consequences if we step out half-cocked. Fear shackles us, and we still sit here with the same problem, although the answer is right around the corner.

"Self-pity comes into our lives and takes a seat. It makes us think somehow our problems are special. It makes us believe that nobody else is suffering or facing the same problem that we have. It tells us to feel sorrow for ourselves. It tells us to mope, to go around telling our friends, telling our relatives, and telling everybody who will lend a listening ear how bad off we are, that fate itself has dealt us a bad blow. We whine, groan, and moan, when all we got to do is go around the corner and find God's answer.

"Some of us are just lazy. God tells us to arise and go forth, trusting in his Word. But we keep putting it off, saying after a while, 'I am going to get up and step out on his Word.' But days go by. Weeks go by. Months go by. Years go by. Life itself may pass, and we may approach the pearly gates with the same problem. All we have to do is arise and step out on his Word."

After reaching his crescendo, after surviving yet another purse attack, Reverend Longmire wiped his brow with a bright white handkerchief, cleaned his spectacles, took a long drink from the glass of water brought to him by Deacon Mike, and stood majestically at the podium. He placed the Bible upright on the podium, placed his water glass on one side, and motioned for a second glass. He then had two water glasses situated on either side of the Bible, standing upright.

He raised one glass in his right hand and set it back down atop the podium while saying, "God gives us problems as gifts so we can grow and learn better to trust in Him." Switching hands, holding the Bible, he raised the second glass in his left hand, saying, "God is a just God.

He never puts on us more than we can bear. He always gives us answers and problems at the same time.

"When we are given problems, we are the ones who put things between us and the answers." Laying the Bible down, flat between the two glasses, he started piling on available items to accentuate his points. Using the Sunday school book, he placed it on top of the Bible, saying, "Pride gets in the way." Sensing what was happening, the assistant pastor handed Reverend Longmire a small Bible, whereupon it was placed atop the large Bible and Sunday school book with the words, "Self-pity gets in the way." Finally, Reverend Longmire placed his own wallet on the growing stack, saying, "Fear, laziness, and a multitude of other excuses come between our God-given problems and God-given answers."

Obviously referring to the storm-splitting incident, Reverend Longmire finally got around to what the packed church had come to hear. "The Bible don't say God only blesses those who go to church. Nor does it say he only answers prayers for those who go to church. He says in Matthew 7:7, 'Ask, and it shall be given you; seek, and you shall find; knock, and it shall be opened unto you.' In the book of Mark, chapter 9, verse 23, 'Jesus said unto him, "If you can believe, all things are possible to him that believes."' The key my brethren"—Reverend Longmire was digging deep and hitting home now—"is that you only believe. If a sinner man or a man known as a sinner goes to God and believes then in him, then all things are possible. Not some things, but all things are possible. A sinner man or a man known as a sinner can raise the dead, heal the sick, and split a storm, if he only believes." The church was a chorus of "amens" as everybody was rocking with Reverend Longmire.

I looked at Mama Rosetta, and she didn't look amused, just shaking her head from side to side with eyes closed and hands clasped just below her waist. I turned my gaze on Papa Mike, who was stoic as a statue. He wasn't agreeing or disagreeing. Just staring.

Me? I was empowered. Henceforth and forever, I would always believe that God Almighty, all-knowing God, is a just God who provides answers to all problems manifested in our lives. We just have to overcome doubt, pride, fear, self-pity, and laziness. What a sermon!

CHAPTER 12

SUNDAY AFTERNOON

Miss Lula's funeral was held at the church on Sunday at 2:00 p.m. Most funerals during prime cotton-chopping or cotton-picking months were held on Sunday. Missing work to bury the dead was not in keeping with the southern way of life where cotton was king. Plantation owners changed Jesus's words in Luke 9:60 to "Let the coloreds bury their own dead on their own time! Their duty is to go and farm this land and raise Kingdom of Cotton!"

Reverend Longmire preached her funeral to a full church. People came from nearby communities who were members of Shady Grove M.B. Church, Pleasant Grove M.B. Church, Woodland M.B. Church, and Silent Grove in Marks. As would be expected, relatives and longtime acquaintances in Chicago, Saint Louis, Detroit, and Memphis were in attendance. These northern cities were the destinations of mass migrations in the 1920s and again in the 1950s. In fact, entire families were relocating on a regular basis. The *Brown v. Board of Education* separate but equal ruling and the steady mechanization of farming were combining to render the coloreds not needed and not wanted.

Only grown-ups were in the choir stand. It was common practice to exclude young people from singing at funerals. This was the time when the senior choir took over, even if only a handful of singers were available. On this day, the choir stand was overloaded with local and visiting choir members, as people were alarmed that a white man had flown a crop duster so low that a black cotton chopper died from a heart attack.

Likewise, the church was full, as the middle pews were reserved for family members. Lots of visitors were claiming kinship in order to get a seat. Those known to local ushers had to stand around the walls, as all seats were taken by the time the program started.

Mama Rosetta was the first to talk about Miss Lula as a member of the mothers' board. She extolled the virtues of a virtuous woman who was faithful to the end. Mama Rosetta was sure Miss Lula was right then and there residing in heavenly bliss with the Father, Son, and the Holy Ghost.

Bro. Luke Lyons spoke of Miss Lula as a neighbor. He shared how generous she was at hog-killing time in assuring that all neighbors had a measure of fresh meat before she stored it in her smokehouse. He, too, was sure that Miss Lula was in a heavenly mansion. She had been sending up her timber all along.

Sis. Katie Randolph, one of several group captains for church dues, was last on the program to make remarks. She shared how Miss Lula always paid her dues promptly and, in accordance with 2 Corinthians 9:7, was a cheerful giver. She quoted verbatim from the King James Version: "Every man according as he purposeth in his heart, so let him give; not grudgingly, or of necessity: for God loveth a cheerful giver."

The presiding officer, or the self-proclaimed mistress of ceremony, Mrs. Sue Ellen McDonald, asked whether anybody else wanted to make a two-minute tribute to Miss Lula. She would take three. As expected, the relatives from "up north" wanted to vent their feelings about white people killing colored people. For after all, Chicago was the home of fourteen-year-old Emmett Till, who was lynched in Money, Mississippi, just two years earlier.

The church grew quiet as not one but three relatives rose and slid between the tight confines of the second row and the third row of relatives. Two oversized men dressed in dark suits and bow ties in their late thirties or early forties stood on either end of the casket, flanking a veiled woman dressed in off-white clothing. The men stood with folded arms and were wearing dark sunglasses. The lady was not wearing glasses, but her face was only visible beneath the veil when looking straight ahead. The church hadn't seen anything near equating to this spectacle.

The lady spoke in soft tones barely above a whisper. She nodded and did a slight bow of the head to the ministers surrounding Reverend Longmire in the pulpit. She looked in the direction of the mistress of ceremony and nodded. Then after what seemed like an eternity, she said, "As-Salaam-Alaikum." Everybody looked futilely from left to right and right to left, trying to figure out what had just been said. No one said a word.

The quiet-spoken woman articulated a long sentence:

"In the Torah, we prescribed for them a life for a life, an eye for an eye, a nose for a nose, an ear for an ear, a tooth for a tooth, an equal wound for a wound: if anyone forgoes this out of charity, it will serve as atonement for his bad deeds. Those who do not judge according to what God has revealed are doing grave wrong (Koran 5:45)."

Then she quoted Pastor Martin Niemöller:

> First they came for the Socialists, and I did not speak out—
> Because I was not a Socialist.
> Then they came for the Trade Unionists, and I did not speak out—
> Because I was not a Trade Unionist.
> Then they came for the Jews, and I did not speak out—
> Because I was not a Jew.
> Then they came for me—and there was no one left to speak for me.

Again, nobody quite understood her jargon or her intentions in saying such words in such flowery language. Yet there was a chorus of "amens" and general encouragement as she spoke.

Finally, the soft-spoken lady said, "Until and unless we do something to stop others from being killed, whether by lynching or scared to death by a low-flying crop-duster airplane, none of us is safe, especially our children. And worst of all, Emmett Till and Cousin Lula will have died in vain."

Then she dropped a bombshell. "We should all take a page out of the sinner's book who split the storm the other day. No matter our circumstances, no matter our respective paths, we should rise to the occasion and do what is needed to be done, when it is to be done and how it is to be done. Forget dangers. Forget what others may say or do. Don't think how big your problem is. Think how big your God is. You and God are a majority. I won't tell you what to do or how to do it, but each of you ought to say, 'If it is to be, it's up to me!'"

She then came back to the second row of the bereaved family section, slid down to the middle, and took her seat. The two oversized, silent men accompanying her went to the third row. The church was stunned momentarily, not knowing whether to agree, disagree, or ignore the call for action. On cue from Reverend Longmire, Mrs. Alice McNutt struck up the piano, and the senior choir rose to sing "Move on up a Little Higher" by Mahalia Jackson. I was deeply enthralled by it all. At last, there was a notion, albeit from a strange up-north "cousin," that something ought to be done to promote justice and fairness for all, as they said about Superman on the radio and on his weekly television show.

Reverend Longmire rose to deliver the eulogy following the rendition by the choir. He spent the first few minutes consoling the bereaved family. He then assured community residents that "God doesn't make mistakes. Everything is unfolding in God's will."

His announced text was Leviticus 19:18, "Vengeance is Mine Saith the Lord." He read from the King James Version: "Thou shalt not avenge, nor bear any grudge against the children of thy people, but thou shalt love thy neighbor as thyself: I am the LORD."

A sense of relief and a near audible sigh swept through the gathered multitude. Somehow, Reverend Longmire was calling for peace and calm and not an armed retaliation. Everyone wanted to retaliate against

Bo Dukes in particular and the white plantation system in particular, but who was going to bell the cat? Everything would be better by and by. Isaiah 40:31 was then read: "But they that wait upon the LORD shall renew their strength; they shall mount up with wings as eagles; they shall run, and not be weary; and they shall walk, and not faint."

The soft-spoken lady with the veil in the second row behind the closest of kin turned to look over her shoulder to the third row and shook her head in disbelief at the oversized, well-dressed accomplice on that side of her. He shrugged his shoulders in an "I told you so" fashion. She then turned to the similarly attired male accomplice on the right, and they repeated the scenario.

I watched and listened from my spot in the front row abutting the deacons' section, where the leading men of the community and nearby communities sat with Papa Mike. Stunned by the challenge issued by the soft-spoken woman, these black leaders rejoiced in the holy words Reverend Longmire was spewing. Yes indeed, the Bible, God's holy Word in Luke 6:28 says, "Bless them that curse you, and pray for them which despitefully use you." Not one mention of the storm splitting was made by anyone. Seemingly, it was a taboo subject.

My personal recourse was to make an appointment to speak to God about all of this. It seemed that something was unjust, unfair, and plain wrong when white folks could misuse and even kill colored folks at will. Surely there was some kind of retribution on this side of hell. Surely there was some explanation of why a sinner had been chosen over a saint to split the storm. Mama's words reverberated in my mind: "We will all understand it better by and by." But when?

CHAPTER 13

"Boy, I heard they burned the Lambert schoolhouse down to the ground!" The words came at me out of nowhere. Deacon Lyons was making a person-to-person pronouncement rather than an announcement during the funeral services for Miss Lula. Somehow, he had missed any small talk about the schoolhouse burning in Lambert. Everybody was talking about the storm splitting, the snake in the Polk salad patch, the airplane spraying, Dimp being hit with a hoe, and of course the passing of Miss Lula. The Lambert Vocational High School had been burned down? Nary a word had I heard until now.

Friendship School across the road from Friendship Missionary Baptist Church was grades one through eight. I had finished the eighth grade and looked forward to enrolling in Lambert High School in July and August for the summer split session. Oh, how I wanted so much to ride the bus with my sister Dimp. This was late April.

Deacon Shelton Lyons and I were the last to leave the church after the repast for Miss Lula. In my duties as church janitor for three dollars a month, I brushed crumbs off the benches and tables onto the floor. Then I quickly but efficiently swept the floor with the straw broom. Deacon Lyons was busily tinkering with the church ledger and talking aloud while trying to balance some figures. He lived in Clarksdale about six miles to the west, while we lived two miles to the east. Deacon Lyons had a car. I was on foot.

"Yeah," Deacon was saying, "I hear they caught some white boy with a kerosene can standing there watching the school burn down to the ground. He didn't even try to get away or hide. Just stood there admiring his work."

I was stunned. Man, I had eagerly anticipated rising the big yellow bus to Lambert for school. My older two sisters had been riding for several years. Now it was my time, and there was no school? I wanted to go to a school where they played baseball and basketball and had a movie projector. My one-through-eight school had absolutely nothing—no electricity, no indoor toilets. Nothing but two teachers, a lot of chairs, two woodstoves, and two outhouses.

I must have been lost in a trance thinking about the burned school and brainstorming about what would happen next.

Deacon Lyons, who spoke loudly as a matter of course, hailed me amid his sweeping with "Hey, boy! They tell me you were with Deacon Mike and Dolph Rhodes when that storm came up last week. What happened?"

So, that's why the deacon was waiting around, tinkering with the ledger. Undaunted, I gave my well-rehearsed response. "I ran and got the ax like Mr. Dolph told me to. I gave it to him, and then I don't know what happened. Lightning flashed, thunder rolled, and everybody fell to the ground. The lightning hurt my eyes, so I shut 'em and fell down like everybody else. When we gathered ourselves and looked up and about, the storm was going 'round, and Mr. Dolph was standing there with the ax in the ground. Papa Mike was right behind him, not real close but right behind him. That's all I know."

Deacon Lyons spoke louder than his usual loudness. "My goodness. That's what I heard. That's what everybody's been telling me all day. Boy, they were even talking about this in Clarksdale. Somebody told me Early Wright mentioned it on the radio. That's big stuff."

"Yes, sir, I imagine." I was trying to be conversant without crossing the line of ambiguity that separated children from adults. I was uncomfortable speaking man-to-man with the deacon. I had never heard of the principle of transactional analysis but I knew all too well that parents-adult-child meant I was on the lower end of the totem pole. When parents or adults spoke, my role was to listen and not voluntarily speak unless asked.

That didn't mean I wasn't thinking ahead and extrapolating the direction and nature of the conversation. I anticipated the deacon's next line of questioning.

"Tell me, boy, what did Deacon Mike do when you gave the ax to Dolph?"

I was intrigued by the deacon's reference to Mr. Dolph Rhodes by just his first name. Choppers in Mama Rosetta's group were always talking and dropping hints that many deacons were secretively patronizing Dolph Rhodes for "toddies." I wondered if Deacon Lyons had stopped by on his visits in that direction to see relatives.

I responded in my rehearsed manner: "I was out of breath from running with the ax and gave it directly to Mr. Dolph. I wasn't looking at anybody else. Papa Mike didn't say anything to my remembrance. Mr. Dolph didn't say anything either. They were standing close together though."

The deacon prodded further. "What happened after the storm split? What did Deacon Mike say? What did he do?"

I had anticipated this oft-asked question and gave my oft-given response. "He stood there a moment like the rest of us, surveying the situation. After it seemed the storm was not going to hit us, he said, 'Get back to work.' That's all I know."

The deacon fired one last volley, trying his best to get the desired response. "Boy, tell me the truth. Was Deacon Mike upset that this sinner-man hoe filer had upstaged him in front of his own wife and hoe hands and split the storm when it was his job to protect and lead, especially in the face of a storm?"

So this was one of those run-on sentences we had tried to outline in English class. I thought for a moment and then said my well-rehearsed response. "Sir, I have no idea. I am scared of lightning, and when it flashed and that loud clap of thunder sounded, I was looking for my mama." Deacon Lyons laughed at that one and decided to let it go.

"Boy, it's getting cloudy out there. I can give you a ride to the four-way turn. That'll help you a little bit on the way home. I don't want any lightning to come up before you get home to your mama."

I was suddenly aware that we were in church. I had not been telling the whole truth and nothing but the truth. I had deliberately withheld my assessment and opinion about the storm-splitting incident. Of course Deacon Lyons was upstaged, upset, and humiliated by the sinner-man hoe flier. But how was a "child" going to stand toe-to-toe with a full-grown deacon in a one-on-one conversation and give an opinion?

I would keep my conclusions to myself. Besides, I was wondering whether they would build another school in Lambert in time for the split summer session.

"Boy, will you drop a handful of these programs off at Dolph Rhodes's on the way home? He didn't come to the funeral, and I know for sure he and his missus thought the world of Miss Bessie." I obliged and accepted five of the programs.

CHAPTER 14

CARDS, DICE, AND MOONSHINE

Being in the presence of Dolph Rhodes away from the cotton fields was unsettling for me. I simply didn't know how to express myself. He was the ultimate sinner. I was a saint in the making.

Dolph Rhodes was every bit sixty years of age. That sounds a lot better than sixty years old. He could have been seventy years old. He wasn't telling, and nobody dared to ask. Everybody was wondering because his common-law wife, Cassie Rhodes, was twenty-seven! Allegedly, he had won her in a card game from her stepfather, George, a compulsive gambler, ex-convict, and major domo at the big house.

Gambling was recreational outlet for those not afraid to incur the wrath of the Lord. Whiskey drinkers were the focus of prayers for mercy at every church service. Those who would dare spend precious dollars (actually, fifty cents per half pint) on intoxicants or wager hard-earned wages were the lowest kind of sinner on this side of murder. Gambling and drinking were sins. The wage of sin is death. Dolph Rhodes bootlegged illegal corn whiskey and ran a gambling operation in his house in full view of his common-law wife and three small children. In the eyes of the churchgoers, Dolph Rhodes was a sinner of the lowest order.

She was a bet won in a crap game. I couldn't believe it at first, but being around Mr. and hearing the gossip day after day, it was becoming real to me. There was whispers in the old ladies cluster that Cassie told them that she'd been won in a crap game. I'd heard that story before, and on this day I believed it.

I was thinking as I neared the house to drop off the funeral programs. Maybe she was the bet "lost" in a card game. Gossip had it that her stepfather had said it was only for a few hours while he went around calling in markers from old debtors. That was eleven years and three children ago. As the story goes, at first she didn't want that old albino man. Things changed. Time changes. Thinking changes. She and Adolph had developed an understanding. She would cook, clean, and do day labor. He would put bread on the table and a roof over her head and occasionally buy her pretty things. While other women, especially wives, were eking out an existence, she and Dolph Rhodes were doing pretty well, thank you very much.

Yet, younger men patronizing their liquor or gaming business or both would invariably make passes at the young bride.

I jumped the ditch as usual and was headed up the walkway toward the front door when I noticed a strange car. It came to me in a flash that the funeral had brought in kit and kin from far and near. This car had a Missouri license plate. A dapper young man, perhaps age thirty, emerged from the vehicle. He wore a leather coat. His hair was processed like Nat King Cole's. He walked into the house ahead of me, as I slowed my pace to allow him to do so. Wasting no time, he walked through the front door, held it open for me, and announced to Dolph Rhodes that he wanted four pints of corn whiskey. Dolph Rhodes nodded his head in agreement, pointed his index finger at me, and sauntered out of the room to get the four pints of corn whiskey. I sat down in a chair near the front door to wait on Dolph Rhodes to return.

The slick-haired stranger caught Cassie's eye and smiled at her.

Dolph Rhodes was the houseman for all gambling bets. He was also bartender and sole salesperson for his stash of corn whiskey. He couldn't keep both hands and eyes on those two operations and watch Cassie at the same time. Cassie knew this. The young Nat King Cole look-alike soon figured the same.

It caught Cassie off guard. She was standing at the woodstove warming leftover turkey and dressing when she felt a tap on her shoulder. As she turned in response to the shoulder tap, he grabbed her and kissed her full on the lips. I slumped in my chair and focused every atom in my being on the typed funeral programs. I read the obituary silently as directed in the copy. I was scared out of my wits. *I see nothing. I hear nothing.* I wasn't about to know anything at all.

I could imagine Cassie hadn't been kissed in eleven years, since she had been won in the crap game. That was surely out of tune with Dolph Rhodes's demeanor and probably skipped in their intimate moments. Surely, her initial reaction was to resist, fight, break free, run. Out of the corner of my eye, I tried not to look but had to. Her resistance lasted a nanosecond or so and then seemed just as quickly to subside.

Maybe her subsequent reaction was not a conscious one but a physical convulsion. Maybe she hadn't been kissed since forever, if ever. Maybe, for eleven years she had longed for such an experience. It flashed through my mind as I pretended to stare at the funeral programs that no way Dolph Rhodes wouldn't have anything of the sort. He had said oftentimes in my presence that the mouth is nasty. "Dogs don't kiss. Mules don't kiss. Chicken don't kiss. Pigs don't kiss. Why should humans go round sucking on one another?" End of discussion.

"What the hell is this? Nigger, I will blow your brains out," Dolph Rhodes hollered out, as he had two pints of liquor in each hand. Quick as a wink, he threw the two in his right hand upside the processed head of what's his name. Cassie bolted through the kitchen door onto the back porch. What's his name was right behind her. Dolph Rhodes had pulled his snub-nosed .38 revolver from his overalls. The first shot sounded loud and thunderous. The bullet hit the number 3 tub on the porch near the top of the steps and ricocheted into the field. I fell flat on the floor. Was this really happening?

What's his name was on the porch and into the cornfield before you could say Jack Robinson. His car was out front. He was headed the opposite direction.

Any second thoughts were overruled by second shots from the snub-nosed .38.

Dolph Rhodes pocketed his pistol and grabbed a broom hanging by the door. He was going to dust his bride—that is, dust his bride with a broomstick. Cassie ran off the porch around the house. My heart was beating like that of rabbits captured during a rundown.

"Come back here, woman. You low-down, backstabbing, dirty ..." Dolph was cussing. He was ambling in what could be called a slow run, but catching Cassie was not about to happen. The young woman circumambulated the house as her common-law husband raved and ranted.

All she could say was "Dolph, nothing happened. Nothing happened. I didn't do it. He made me." She was denying, contradicting, and admitting all in one breath. I dared not breathe, let alone move. No way was I going to get in the way of a domestic dispute.

Several of the gamblers, attracted by the resulting ruckus, collared Dolph Rhodes and wrestled him to the ground. It didn't take much; he was already out of breath. I got my breath and announced, "Mr. Dolph, I brought you some funeral programs. I am leaving them on the table." As it seemed lately all I had been doing was making fast tracks, I started running down the brick walkway, over the dredge ditch, onto the gravel road, and toward home.

I could hear one loud-talking man trying to convince Dolph Rhodes that Cassie was a faithful and devoted wife. Whatever happened was not her fault. "All right, all right, I ain't gonna hurt her," Dolph Rhodes was rasping. "Give me back my gun."

I guess, having worked up a dander, he needed some sort of relief. Seemingly, his wrath turned to the stranger who had the audacity to violate the sanctity of his castle. I could imagine Dolph Rhodes walking to the front of the house and peering into the empty blackness. Seeing nothing, he would seethe even more. Then my heart skipped a beat or two. Gunshots pierced the night air. Perhaps convinced that his wife had been attacked, Dolph Rhodes must have emptied the chambers of his snub-nosed .38 into the side of the green 1952 Chevrolet parked in front of his house. I heard Dolph Rhodes holler, "Where is that black

Yankee? What's his name is going back to Saint Louis with holes in his car. Humph, that's better than holes in his hide." That was the second "air-conditioned" car owned by a colored man in the community. Jessie Blue's 1953 Mercury was the first.

Wheezing mightily, wringing wet with sweat, and scared out of my mind, I finally made it home. Funny how quaint, even sad-looking houses can be so homely. As soon as I slowed my pace to ease into the back door and into the boys' room, I felt that warm, fuzzy feeling. There is no place like home.

CHAPTER 15

Thou shalt not tempt the Lord thy God.
—Deuteronomy 6:16

It is also written: "Do not put the Lord your God to the test."
—Matthew 4:7

Papa Mike, Dolph Rhodes, and I lived in a one, two, three arrangement respectively, on the same stretch of road, with each separated by a third of a mile. Deacon Lyons had given me a ride covering the first mile of the two-mile walk home from church. The ride placed me within a hundred yards of Papa Mike's residence.

I glanced at Papa Mike's house as he got out of the car and headed for home. The clouds, as Robert Frost would say, were low and hairy in the skies. Lightning flashed in the distance. I broke into my customary trot, or as my brother Bob in the air force called it, double time.

I heard the familiar sound of a slow-moving car approaching from the rear and instinctively moved closer to the dredge ditch on the right-hand side of the gravel road. Older colored people and well-to-do white people, especially white women, drove slowly. The few young colored people privileged to drive anybody's cars, theirs or the boss's, drove at rapid paces. Young white boys drove like bats out of Hades. So, this car was an older person. I wondered who it was and whether that person, if colored, would kindly give me a ride. The lightning was getting fierce. Not that everybody should know, especially Joker and the signifying bunch, but I was getting scared. Real scared.

The voice was all too familiar. "Water Boy, get in this car." It was Papa Mike. Relieved, jubilant, and feeling rescued, I happily obliged. I opened the front door of the roadster and, feeling a slight discomfort, sat in the passenger's seat next to the boss man.

Papa Mike had both hands on the steering wheel. He was dressed in his cotton chopper's overseer khakis with his cotton chopper's overseer hat on as well. He was talking idly. "Looks like a storm is brewing. Mama Rosetta checked *Farmers' Almanac*, and it sho nuff said we'd have a storm on the fifth Sunday."

Having just left the church where there had been a funeral, a burial, and a repast, I knew full well it was the fifth Sunday. In fact, I was still dressed in my Sunday best, albeit a somewhat crumpled hand-me-down blue dress jacket and almost-too-short gray slacks. I had on brown lace-up Sunday loafers that were much too small but felt much better since they burst at the seams below the laces. Surprisingly, Papa Mike had changed from his black funeral suit and was already dressed for Monday.

The car slowed even more as it pulled up in front of Dolph Rhodes's house. A fleeting thought was, *Papa Mike is confused. He thinks this is my house.* Before the words were rehearsed to be spoken—I always rehearsed words before speaking to grown-ups—the answer came. "I am going inside and ask Adolph to ride with us. You can sit in the back seat."

Within a matter of a few minutes, the two men emerged from the house and came walking up the walkway toward the parked car. Normally, Dolph Rhodes patronized gamblers and whiskey drinkers on Sundays. This time, he had served notice that he was going to Miss Lula's funeral, and nobody should come to his house for anything. The word apparently got around. Nobody was there, or so it seemed from the outside. Lightning flashed, and the silhouette of the two men flashed in a double shadow across the front of the house. The following peel of thunder cackled and rolled. This smacked of secrecy. "What in the world are we about to do?"

Mr. Dolph spoke in hushed tones as usual but with some degree of eeriness that emitted trepidation. I began thinking about Carl Jung's definition of *intuition* as "perception via the unconscious: using sense-perception only as a starting point, to bring forth ideas, images, possibilities, ways out of a blocked situation, by a process that is mostly unconscious." Intuitively, I was getting scared of being with these two men at this time.

Papa Mike made fear omnipresent when he said, "We are going back to that same cotton field where the storm caught the choppers the other day. I am going to split the storm this time. I want you two there with me."

When humans are set upon with an unfavorable occurrence, they may go through shock, disbelief, denial, self-pity, and anger and just may arrive at acceptance. After acceptance, then and only then can humans arrive at the healthy stage of coping.

I went rapidly through shock, disbelief, and denial and stopped squarely at self-pity or "Why me?" I knew better than to be angry. Papa Mike was the head of the deacons' board and the boss of the cotton choppers crew. Plus, Papa Mike was the most respected colored man in the community. My perspective of the return engagement announcement moved slowly and reluctantly to acceptance, draped ever so elegantly in fear of the unknown. As usual, I was real scared.

Dolph Rhodes said nary a word. He sat slumped-shouldered on the passenger side as the roadster rambled past my mama's house. The lights were on. The curtains were partially closed on the west side.

"Water Boy, we will be back in a jiffy. Your mama won't be worried for long. You are in good hands," Papa Mike said reassuringly as they went on past my house, on past Mr. Eddie's house, and to the cotton field where the event occurred.

The roadster pulled off the gravel road onto the packed dirt of the turn road. Dust was billowing now as we slowly approached the quadrant of cotton field where the storm splitting occurred. "Let's get out here and see what happens," Papa Mike directed.

Obediently, I, the water boy, and the hoe filer both exited the roadster. Papa Mike, in a deliberate and unhurried manner, got out, walked around to the back of his car, and opened the trunk. He took out a pair of cowhide work gloves with the striped topsides and plain insides.

With gloves firmly pulled on, he reached inside the car trunk and retrieved a Barco Kelly Woodslasher Michigan double-bit ax!

He said, "Water Boy, on second thoughts, you can sit in the car and watch. Adolph and I will do what we have to do out here."

Dolph Rhodes still was closemouthed but cooperative. Seems as if he and Papa Mike had some kind of understanding. Maybe they had talked. Or maybe they just understood.

Out of harm's way, I looked on in amazement and wonderment from the back seat of the roadster. It was becoming evident that another episode of storm splitting was about to take place. My goodness, Papa Mike was looking for redemption and self-effacement after having been defaced. It was becoming clear that I was a mere witness. What was Mr. Dolph's role?

Whatever was going to take place had better be quick. According to the National Weather Service:

> If you are outside and there are thunderstorms within 10 miles, you are at risk of being struck. In rare cases, lightning has been known to travel as far as 15 miles from the storm. There are four different types of lightning: Within cloud, cloud-to-cloud, cloud-to-air, and cloud-to-ground. Lightning can occur from any portion of the thunderstorm cloud. Thunderstorms can extend up to 10 miles high in the atmosphere and they are often tilted by stronger winds aloft. High clouds above, you may be part of a thunderstorms anvil. Often during the dissipating stage of a thunderstorm, lightning will strike from the upper reaches of the storm, including the anvil.

Papa Mike, realizing that arrival of the approaching storm was imminent, was praying aloud with his left hand on the ax and his right hand on the shoulder of a reticent and obliging Dolph Rhodes. The sound of thunder and the distance of the two men from the roadster rendered hearing all but impossible. Overcome with curiosity, I rolled down the back window so I could hear. The cool wind from the oncoming storm and soft raindrops rushed inside to join me. Raindrops splattered my face.

I could barely hear Papa Mike, but putting two and two together to make sense of the situation, I trembled with a mixture of excitement and fear. Papa Mike was tempting the Lord thy God. He was putting the Lord God to the test. He wanted to show the sinner man that God Almighty would respond to the beseeching of a head deacon at the church.

"Oh God, I call upon you on behalf of your church, your children of the church here and everywhere, to show your might to this sinner man and all nonbelievers."

Papa Mike, invoking the Trinitarian formula of "in the name of the Father, Son, and Holy Ghost," reared back with both hands on the handle, fully intending to plunge the double-bit ax into the soft earth. He never made it.

Mother Nature and Mother Earth conspired and combined to punish both the vocal deacon and the silent sinner at the same time. As I watched the storm rush toward us, I had no idea of what a meteorologist might have to say. Yet, looking back on it now, I do know what the National Weather Service says about the dangers of lightning.

> The National Weather Service advises: An entire lightning strike employs both upward and downward moving forces. However, the return stroke of a lightning bolt travels from the ground into the cloud and accounts for more that 99% of the luminosity of a lightning strike. What is seen by the naked eye as lightning does indeed travel from the ground into the cloud.

Lying flat on the ground was once thought to be the best course of action, but this advice is now decades out of date. When lightning strikes the earth, it induces currents in the ground that can be fatal up to 100 feet away. These currents fan out from the strike center in a tendril pattern, so in order to minimize your chance of being struck, you have to minimize both your height and your body's contact with the earth's surface.

The deacon and the sinner were not aware of this. Nor did it matter. The upraised handheld ax served as a lightning rod or something close to it. A bolt of lightning, or something close to it, lit up the ax at the pinnacle of its arc while raised aloft. Its blades shone bright red in the murkiness of the cloudy evening light. The double-bladed ax bounded from the hands of the deacon and simply disappeared into the dusk.

The worst kind of lightning experience is a direct strike. Statistically, it's the most fatal.

The ground around them, and beneath the roadster, trickled and vibrated with electrical shock waves. Both men went sprawling across rows of cotton in tandem as if they were dual manifestations of some meteoric message from on high. They landed in a tangle of legs and arms, holding on to each other like Siamese twins.

Scared out of my wits, most unlike superhero role models, I hunkered down on the floorboard of the roadster with a vivid recollection of the two men still moving and not lifeless. I dared not get up and look immediately. I just stayed down and prayed. I recited the words of Jesus as he hung on the cross: "Father, forgive them; for they know not what they do. Surely, they do not know any better to tempt or test the Lord their God." I wasn't through. I then recited the Lord's Prayer. Finally, fortified with prayerful assurances, I rose and looked out of the car window.

Dolph Rhodes and Papa Mike were walking laboriously, arm in arm, helping each other in slow, painstaking steps toward the roadster. In the approaching dusk, they were drenched in rainwater but literally glowing and silhouetted in the redness of the setting sun visible on the horizon behind a gap in the V-shaped storm. My God, the storm had split!

Intrigued, I mustered up enough courage to get out into the heavy downpour and open both front doors of the roadster. Whatever they had tried to prove, stopping the storm or splitting the storm, apparently happened.

I helped Dolph Rhodes get into the front seat first since the men came from that side. Mr. Dolph smelled the telltale stench of burned clothing. Burned anything in that torrential downpour seemed contradictory. Yet it was unmistakably the odor of burned clothing. I wondered whether there was burned flesh as well. I decided there was not.

Papa Mike was almost inside the car when I eventually made it around to that side to lend a hand. Again, there was the smell of burned clothing. A cursory glance revealed that Papa Mike's gloves were seared and rent into stringy tatters. I dared not look any closer. Too much information is sometimes too much to bear.

The roadster moved on the rain-soaked turn road with little difficulty. The packed earth was slick but unyielding as the rain came down in torrents. Moaning and coughing, Papa Mike steered the vehicle back to the gavel road and headed back west. This time, the one, two, three order of our houses over the mile-long stretch was me, Dolph Rhodes, and Papa Mike.

I wanted to get home fast. I was still dumbfounded as to what the two men had accomplished or not accomplished. Surely, Papa Mike had wanted to prove that a saint had more sway with the Almighty than a sinner. What was Mr. Dolph's motive? His goal?

Nobody was talking as the roaster traveled the short distance from the cotton fields to my mama's home, where our family was surely worried about me. As if on cue, I began rehearsing a question to ask before exiting. Again, I never got the chance.

Papa Mike started talking. "Water Boy, God is the God of everything and everybody. God works in mysterious ways. His wonders to perform. He said, 'My thoughts are not your thoughts, and my ways are not your ways … For as the heavens are higher than the earth, so are my ways higher than your ways and my thoughts than your thoughts.'"

As I opened the car door to depart their company, Dolph Rhodes spoke for the first time since his mumbled greetings when he first started this trip. "In John 13:7, Jesus tells his disciples, 'You do not know now what I am doing, but later, you will understand.'" Now that was a shocker. Dolph Rhodes, the self-avowed sinner man, was quoting scripture, albeit sounding slightly inaccurate.

"Mike, what time Sunday school starts? I have always wanted to be a Sunday school teacher."

Dolph Rhodes and Papa Mike were oblivious of me as I slid out the back door and closed it quietly behind me.

I hurried up the rocky walkway, vaulted the steps, and was on the porch when there at the opened front door I saw Mama waiting anxiously. A final thought came to mind, and I looked back to ask about the whereabouts of the ax, but the roadster was pulling off. The storm was now obviously splitting, draping the setting sun. Maybe it was symbolic that the two colleagues had buried the hatchet … er double-bit ax. I wondered what Lillian was doing. Was Ollie Mae warm and dry? Was Cupcake still thinking of me? After the storm blew over, it would be back to the fields Monday morning.

Printed in the United States
By Bookmasters